MORMON
FUNDAMENTALISM

Cover: The Angel Moroni statue, on top of many Mormon temples, portrays the ancient prophet who quoted verses from Malachi to Joseph Smith that Christ would come to his temple in the last days. Gender symbols portray one man joined to two women in a polygamous relationship. Plural marriage is the most prominent different between Mormon fundamentalists and members of the Church of Jesus Christ of Latter-day Saints.

SETTING THE RECORD STRAIGHT

MORMON FUNDAMENTALISM

Brian C. Hales

Millennial Press, Inc.
P.O. Box 1741
Orem, UT 84059

ISBN: 1-932597-56-1

Copyright © 2008 Millennial Press

Cover design and typesetting by Adam Riggs

Dedication

To Lee and Barbara Hales,
shining examples and loving parents.

Contents

Acknowledgments

I express appreciation to J. Max Anderson, Ron Barney, Alex Baugh, Don Bradley, Lavina Fielding Anderson, and Greg Kofford, and several unnamed Mormon fundamentalists and former Mormon fundamentalists, for their assistance and encouragement. Thanks to Randy Bott, Lindsey Shumway, Martha Parker, Adam Riggs, and the rest of the Millennial Press group for their excellent and expeditious work. I am especially grateful to my four children for their friendship, love, and support.

Preface

In 1989, I received a phone call from my father informing me that my sister had joined the Allred polygamy group and had been excommunicated from the Church. At my request, she shared with me pamphlets and books that she had read that led her to change her religious convictions.

My response, however, was different from hers. In short, I could never feel comfortable with their claims to priesthood authority, and I took D&C 132:18 seriously—without proper authority, plural marriages "are not valid." I researched their teachings further and in 1992, with the help of J. Max Anderson, published *The Priesthood of Modern Polygamy: An LDS Perspective*, which discussed several of my concerns, on a vanity press.

The years rolled by, and in 2003, just as the Warren Jeffs saga was building up steam, I sensed a need for someone to write a history of the Mormon fundamentalist movement. With the help of publisher Greg Kofford and editor Lavina Fielding Anderson, I wrote *Modern Polygamy and Mormon Fundamentalism: The Generations After the Manifesto* (Greg Kofford Books, 2006). It took three years to complete the book, which has over 500 pages, 2000 endnotes, 400 references, and 100 illustrations. While it certainly is

not the final word on Mormon fundamentalism, it hopefully increases the accessibility of useful information regarding the movement for both polygamists and LDS Church members alike. It received the "Best Book of 2007 Award" from the John Whitmer Historical Association.

This paperback, *Setting the Record Straight: Mormon Fundamentalism*, is in many ways a "Cliff Notes" version of my earlier volume. Whole chapters have been condensed to a single sentence or paragraph. If an inquirer has additional questions or interest, he or she might benefit from reading the expanded version. In addition, this book has sections dealing with questions and doctrinal differences between the Mormon fundamentalists and The Church of Jesus Christ of Latter-day Saints.

This volume is different from *Modern Polygamy and Mormon Fundamentalism: The Generations After the Manifesto*, which was written as an invitation to Mormon fundamentalists to study their own history and beliefs and perhaps to join or rejoin the Church of Jesus Christ of Latter-day Saints. In contrast, this book is designed as a warning to LDS Church members regarding teachings that I believe to be untrue, and therefore incapable of bringing eternal happiness. Regardless, I do not wish for its tone or conclusions to be offensive in any way to Mormon fundamentalists who are generally very good people, devout and sincere in their convictions. Neither do I wish to offend anyone who wishes to disagree with me on any of the topics discussed. I would happily defend their right to believe according to their own consciences and hope they would afford me the same benefit.

In writing about Mormon fundamentalists, I am aware that they prefer to be called "fundamentalist Mormons." In choosing the terms I use, I do not wish to convey any disrespect. Yet, for me, a true "fundamentalist Mormon" would embrace the whole of the Church's fundamental teachings, not just a specialized version of one or two principles, and the need for proper priesthood authority to perform valid ordinances, including baptism, would exclude freelance baptisms (those performed without genuine authority) as a gateway to becoming "Mormons." These two concerns limit my ability to refer to "Mormon fundamentalists" as "fundamentalist Mormons." All major religions have "fundamentalist" factions attached to them, and the Mormon variety shares many parallels with their counterparts of other spiritual traditions. In that context, they easily qualify as "Mormon fundamentalists."

Brian C. Hales, May 2008

Chronology

1831

Joseph Smith learns that plural marriage can be acceptable to God.

1834

An angel appears to Joseph Smith, commanding him to practice plural marriage.

1835

Joseph Smith marries his first plural wife, Fanny Alger. The marriage dissolves quickly.

1836

Sealing authority is restored through a visitation from the Old Testament Prophet Elijah in the Kirtland Temple.

1841

Joseph Smith begins plural marriage anew in Nauvoo.

1842

Other men in Nauvoo become polygamists.

1844

Joseph Smith is martyred; Brigham Young becomes the key holder of sealing authority.

1852

Brigham Young announces the previously secret practice of polygamy to the world.

1862

The U.S. government passes the first federal legislation against polygamy.

1877

Brigham Young dies, and John Taylor becomes the "one" man holding the sealing keys.

1882

Additional federal laws are passed against plural marriage.

1887

John Taylor passes away, leaving Wilford Woodruff as the "one" man.

1889

More federal legislation against polygamy.

1890

The "Manifesto" is presented by Wilford Woodruff telling the Saint that plural marriage is no longer *commanded* by God. Plural marriages are still secretly *permitted*.

1899

Wilford Woodruff dies. Lorenzo Snow becomes President of the Church and the "one."

1902

Lorenzo Snow passes on. Joseph F. Smith becomes the key holder and President of the Church.

1904

President Smith issues the "second manifesto." Thereafter new plural marriages are *not permitted*.

1904–20s

Scattered individuals attempt their own plural marriages without the permission of the President of the Church and are excommunicated. No organized groups or leaders exist.

1912

Lorin Woolley writes an account saying that in 1886, John Taylor received a visit from Joseph Smith while staying in the Woolley home.

1914

Lorin Woolley's father, patriarch John W. Woolley, is excommunicated for performing plural marriages. He claims apostle Matthias Cowley gave him authorization.

1918

Joseph F. Smith dies. President of the Church Heber J. Grant holds the sealing keys.

1921

John Woolley's son, Lorin, remembers that back in 1886, he and four other men were ordained with authority to seal plural marriages independent of the Church. None of the other men leave any similar record.

1920s

Polygamists band together for meetings but without any identifiable leaders.

1921

Joseph Musser is excommunicated for plural marriage.

1921–34

Lorin Woolley tells many stories. He expands his 1912 account, saying that in 1886, there was an eight-hour meeting with thirteen individuals in attendance. Reportedly, a "manifesto" to discontinue plural marriage was discussed and vigorously rejected. Lorin claimed that he was afterwards ordained to a previously unheard of office of "High Priest Apostle" and made a member of a previously unheard of priesthood quorum, "The Council of Seven Friends."

1925

Monogamist Lorin Woolley is excommunicated for telling lies about Church leaders.

1928

John Woolley dies outside of the Church, having lived as a polygamist (with two wives) for only six years of his life (1886–1892).

1929

Charles W. Kingston is excommunicated for polygamy.

1929–34

Lorin Woolley calls six other men to fill his "Council of Seven Friends": J. Leslie Broadbent, John Y. Barlow, Joseph W. Musser, Charles F. Zitting, LeGrand Woolley, and Louis Kelsch. They assert authority over the Church. President Heber J. Grant ignores their claims.

1933–34

Woolley, Broadbent, Barlow, and Musser publish three booklets describing their priesthood organization. Most polygamists unite under them without ascribing to all of their ideas.

1934

Lorin Wolley dies. J. Leslie Broadbent becomes the leader of the Council of Seven Friends.

1934

J. Leslie Broadbent ordains Elden Kingston with undisclosed priesthood authority.

1935

Broadbent succumbs to pneumonia. John Y. Barlow assumes leadership over the Council of Friends. *Truth* magazine is started by Joseph Musser. Musser and Barlow visit Short Creek, Arizona. Polygamists are arrested.

1935

Elden Kingston, son of Charles W. Kingston, reports receiving visits from angelic messengers giving him knowledge and power.

1836

John Y. Barlow is asked if he holds the sealing keys and answers in the negative. Musser explains that he also doesn't know where the keys are located.

1941

John Y. Barlow calls and ordains new "High Priest Apostles."

1941

Elden Kingston organizes the Davis Council Cooperative Society.

1942

The United Effort Plan (UEP) is started in Short Creek, Arizona.

1944

Law enforcement officials conduct a raid, arresting fifteen men who are convicted and incarcerated the next year.

1945

Eleven of the fifteen men sign a "manifesto" agreeing to abandon plural marriage and are paroled after six months.

1945

Heber J. Grant passes away, and George Albert Smith becomes President of the Church.

1948

Elden Kingston dies. His brother Ortell Kingston leads the Kingston organization.

1949

John Y. Barlow dies, having added seven new members to the Council of Seven Friends during his tenure. The Council now contains eleven High Priest Apostles. Musser assumes the senior position.

1950

Joseph Musser ignores the seniority of the other ten members of the Council of Friends (commonly called the "Priesthood Council") and ordains Rulon C. Allred as his successor.

1950

A. Dayer LeBaron dies. His children and wife testify that he had special priesthood authority. Joel LeBaron claims angelic visitations and authority from his father.

1951

David O. Mckay becomes President of the Church and sealing key holder.

1952

Rebellion occurs among Priesthood Council members who refuse to accept Rulon C. Allred. Musser releases the old Council and calls seven new Council members (seldomly referred to as High Priest Apostles by this time). A split occurs with Musser and Rulon Allred presiding in Salt Lake City over the new Priesthood Council, and Leroy Johnson presiding in Short Creek. Charles Zitting, LeGrand Woolley, and Louis Kelsch refuse to be involved.

1953

State officials raid Short Creek, apprehending 122 adults and 263 children. The men are quickly charged, convicted, and paroled. The mothers are allowed to accompany their children and are sent to foster homes but eventually released. Three years later, all have returned to Short Creek.

1954

Musser, who had been incapacitated by several strokes, dies. Rulon Allred presides.

1955

Joel LeBaron files papers of incorporation for the Church of the Firstborn with the State of Utah. His brother incorporates the Church of the Firstborn of the Fullness of Times. Both claim authority from their father.

1970

Joseph Fielding Smith becomes the new President of the Church and "one" man holding the sealing keys.

1971

Ervil LeBaron organizes his own Church of the Lamb of God.

1972

Ervil LeBaron sends followers who kill his brother Joel.

1972

Harold B. Lee becomes President of the Church and controller of sealing authority.

1973

Spencer W. Kimball succeeds Harold B. Lee.

1975

The Allred Group incorporates themselves and the Apostolic United Brethren or AUB.

1977

Rulon Allred is shot by followers of Ervil LeBaron. Owen Allred becomes the new AUB leader. Ervil is prosecuted and incarcerated.

1981

Ervil LeBaron dies in prison.

1983

The state of Utah sues Ortell Kingston for welfare subsidies fraud. He pays $250,000, and the case is dropped.

1984

Leroy Johnson releases Priesthood Council members Marion Hammon and Alma Timpson (called years before by John Y. Barlow). They split off to form Centennial Park.

1984

Ron and Dan Lafferty murder their sister-in-law and her daughter.

1985

Ezra Taft Benson become President of the Church and the "one" man.

1986

Leroy Johnson passes away. Rulon Jeffs becomes leader. They incorporate as the FLDS Church.

1987

Ortell Kingston dies. His son Paul Elden Kingston assumes the leadership role.

1994

Howard W. Hunter is the new President of the Church and holder of the sealing keys.

1995

Gordon B. Hinckley succeeds Howard W. Hunter.

1999

David Ortell Kingston is convicted for incest, and John Daniel Kingston is convicted for felony child abuse.

2000

Jeremy Ortell Kingston is convicted of incest in his marriage to his fifteen-year-old cousin. Tom Green is convicted of bigamy and criminal non-support.

2002

Rulon Jeffs dies. Not believing in a Priesthood Council of any size, neither Jeffs or Johnson, called new members. The leadership vacuum is filled by Warren Jeffs, who had been his incapacitated father's spokesman for several years.

2002

Brian David Mitchell kidnaps Elizabeth Smart.

2003

Warren Jeffs excommunicates all potential rivals. He acquires land in Eldorado, Texas.

2005

FLDS temple in Eldorado, Texas is dedicated. Warrant for Warren Jeffs' arrest is issued.

2005

Owen Allred dies, and J. LaMoine Jenson succeeds him as leader of the AUB.

2006

Warren Jeffs hides and is placed on the FBI's Ten Most Wanted List. Later he is arrested.

2007

Warren Jeffs is convicted of two counts of rape as an accomplice. He also abdicates his position as prophet of the FLDS Church.

2008

Thomas S. Monson becomes President of the LDS Church and the "one" man holding all sealing keys.

2008

Texas law enforcement officials raid the Eldorado compound, taking over 400 children into state custody.

Questions Regarding Mormon Fundamentalists and their Doctrines

This section contains questions identifying a number of significant doctrinal differences between The Church of Jesus Christ of Latter-day Saints and the Mormon fundamentalist factions. Since Mormon fundamentalist doctrines vary from group to group and often from individual to individual, the representations presented here cannot be completely generalized.

1. *Mormon fundamentalists believe that polygamy is required by God today. Is that true?*
2. *Mormon fundamentalists believe that plural marriage is required for exaltation. Is that true?*
3. *Mormon fundamentalists believe that the more wives they marry in mortality, the greater their eternal reward. Is this a true doctrine?*
4. *Mormon fundamentalists marry teenagers and have families with females as young as fourteen. Did early Church leaders and members follow this practice?*
5. *Mormon fundamentalists believe section 132 of the Doctrine and Covenants is strictly about polygamy. Is that true?*
6. *Mormon fundamentalists believe that God's directive to "Go... and do the works of Abraham" in section*

132:32 is a specific command to practice plural marriage. Is that true?

7. What priesthood authority to Mormon fundamentalists claim to exercise when performing their marriages?

8. What about the Adam-God theory? What is more fundamental, the teachings of Joseph Smith and the scriptures regarding the identity of Adam, or ideas that were never fully explained that came afterwards?

9. Does God expect us to live the law of consecration now?

10. Some Mormon fundamentalist leaders exercise immense control over property, homes, marriages, and families of their followers. Did Joseph Smith, Brigham Young, John Taylor, and other Church leaders behave that way?

11. Some Mormon fundamentalists seem comfortable using deception to defraud the government of welfare subsidies. Have Church leaders ever encouraged men to marry plural wives they could not support?

12. Mormon fundamentalists do no missionary work. Is it possible that God would exempt any of His followers from this fundamental responsibility?

13. Historically, Mormon fundamentalists have done little or no temple work to save the dead. Is it possible that they are exempted from this fundamental work?

1. Mormon fundamentalists believe that polygamy is required by God today. Is that true?

A review of religious history shows that polygamy may be commanded, permitted, or not permitted by God according to "the circumstances, responsibilities, and personal... duties of the people of God" in their respective ages.[1]

When Joseph Smith first learned in the early 1830s that polygamy as practiced by Old Testament patriarchs had been acceptable to God, he was still *not permitted* to enter into it.[2] However, within a few years he and other Church members were *permitted*, but it was not then required of all Latter-day Saints. In 1852, the principle was taught publicly and for thirty-eight years plural marriage was considered a *commandment*. The 1890 Manifesto removed the commandment, but history shows that polygamy was still *permitted* until 1904. Thereafter, plural marriage was (and is) *not permitted*. These directives have all been administered through the "one" man who holds the keys of sealing authority in an orderly way (D&C 132:8, 18).

In 1891, First Counselor in the First Presidency George Q. Cannon explained: "The Nephites [in the Book of Mormon], according to all that has come down to us, were monogamists. This law was not given to them, as far as we have any account. Yet they were a great and a mighty people before the Lord."[3]

---

1. Joseph F. Smith, in *Journal of Discourses*, 26 vols. (Liverpool: F. D. Richards, 1855–86), 20:28–29, July 7, 1878.

2. According to Orson Pratt, in 1869, Joseph Smith "told individuals, then in the Church that he had inquired of the Lord concerning the principles of plurality of wives, and he received for answer that the principle of taking more wives than one is a true principle, but the time had not yet come for it to be practiced." (Orson Pratt, in *Journal of Discourses*, 13:193, October 7, 1869.)

3. George Q. Cannon, in Brian H. Stuy, ed. and comp., *Collected Discourses* 5 vols. (Burbank, Calif.: B.H.S. Publishing, 1987–92), 2:294. See also Orson Pratt, in *Journal of Discourses,* 6:351 and 13:192, July 4, 1859 and October 7, 1869; H. W. Naisbitt, in *Journal of Discourses*, 26:115, March 8, 1885.

To Jacob in the Book of Mormon, God stated that, depending upon His will and earthly circumstances, "I will command my people" (see Jacob 2:27–30) regarding their marriage practices, usually specifying monogamy, but at other times permitting or commanding polygamy.[4]

God's marital laws are regulated by Him through the "one" man who holds the keys. The opinions and desires of other men and women are of no consequence. Church members today believe the President of the Church is the "one" holding the sealing authority, and he has taught that plural marriage is not permitted.

2. Mormon fundamentalists believe that plural marriage is required for exaltation. Is that true?

Throughout religious history, only one group of God's followers were required to practice plural marriage, and then for only thirty-eight years: the Latter-day Saints between 1852 and 1890. Nevertheless, many Mormon fundamentalists today believe that plural matrimony is still (and always will be) required for exaltation. Concerning this possibility, George Q. Cannon taught one year after the 1890 Manifesto:

> I know there are a great many who feel that, this being a principle of exaltation, they may be in danger of losing their exaltation, because of their inability to obey this. I want to say to all such that the Lord judges our hearts; He looks at our motives. There were a great many men in past times who never had the privilege of obeying this doctrine, because the law was not given to them. Do you think that they are excluded from exaltation? Do you think that they will be deprived of celestial glory? I do not.[5]

---

4. Brian C. Hales, *Modern Polygamy and Mormon Fundamentalism: the Generations after the Manifesto* (Salt Lake City: Greg Kofford Books, 2006), 77–96.
5. George Q. Cannon, in *Collected Discourses*, 2:294.

Similarly, while serving as the "one" man in 1901, President Lorenzo Snow instructed:

> "Some of the brethren are worrying about the matter and feel that they ought to have other wives. Brethren, do not worry; you will lose nothing." Turning to Heber, he said, "There is Brother Heber J. Grant, who is without a son and who consequently feels anxious about it." I want to say to Brother Grant that he will have sons and daughters and his posterity shall become as numerous as the sands upon the seashore or the stars in heaven—the promise made to Abraham is his through faithfulness. Brethren, don't worry about these things, and if you don't happen to secure the means you would like, don't feel disappointed. The Lord will make you rich in due time, and if you are faithful, you will become Gods in eternity. This I know to be the truth."[6]

Brigham Young agreed:

> A man may embrace the Law of Celestial Marriage in his heart and not take the second wife and be justified before the Lord."[7]
>
> If you desire with all your hearts to obtain the blessings which Abraham obtained, you will be polygamists at least in your faith, or you will come short of enjoying the salvation and the glory which Abraham has obtained."[8]
>
> The doctrine of plurality of wives was revealed to this people from heaven, and if heaven had revealed that we should have no wife at all, it would have been as faithfully observed as the present law, even if it should result in the depopulation of the world.[9]

6. Stan Larson, ed., *A Ministry of Meetings: The Apostolic Diaries of Rudger Clawson* (Salt Lake City: Signature Books, 1993), 300–01.

7. Quoted in Wilford Woodruff, *Wilford Woodruff's Journal, 1833–1898, Typescript*, ed. Scott G. Kenney, 9 vols. (Midvale, Utah: Signature Books, 1983–84), entry for September 24, 1871.

8. Brigham Young, in *Journal of Discourses*, 11:268–69, August 19, 1866.

9. Ibid.

If it is necessary to have two wives, take them. If it is right, reasonable and proper and the Lord permits a man to take half a dozen wives, take them; but if the Lord says let them alone, let them alone. How long? Until we go down to the grave, if the Lord demand it.[10]

I would be willing to give up half or two-thirds of my wives, or to let the whole of them go, if it was necessary, if those who should take them would lead them to eternal salvation… Would I get more wives? if I had a mind to; but if I had none at all it would be all right. If I have one it is all right, and if I should have a score it would be all right.[11]

If it is wrong for a man to have more than one wife at a time, the Lord will reveal it by and by, and he will put it away that it will not be known in the Church.[12]

If we could make every man upon the earth get him a wife, live righteously and serve God, we would not be under the necessity, perhaps, of taking more than one wife. But they will not do this; the people of God, therefore, have been commanded to take more wives.[13]

Apostle John Henry Smith recalled that "President Young once proposed that we marry but one wife."[14]

No priesthood leader has ever taught that all men in the celestial kingdom are polygamists or that plural marriage is required for exaltation, irrespective of where and when a person has lived. The whole concept is foreign to Book of Mormon teachings and God's promises to His children. In addition, requiring all exalted men to be polygamists would necessitate at least twice as many women as men in the celestial kingdom. It appears that women have a greater propensity to embrace

10. Brigham Young, in *Journal of Discourses,* 14:160–61, June 4, 1871.
11. Ibid., 12:263, August 9, 1868.
12. Ibid., 11:268, August 19, 1866.
13. Ibid., 16:166–67, August 31, 1873.
14. Anthon H. Lund, Diary, January10, 1900 as found in "LDS Church Authority and New Plural Marriages, 1890–1904," *Dialogue: A Journal of Mormon Thought* 18 (Spring 1985): 26.

spiritual things, but will the ratio be at least two women to each man? Some modern polygamists teach that men should seek more than just two wives. Believing that all exalted men are practicing polygamists generates logistical problems that are not easily resolved.

3. Mormon fundamentalists believe that the more wives they marry in mortality, the greater their eternal reward. Is this a true doctrine?

Mormon fundamentalists generally believe that the more wives a man marries on earth, the greater his exaltation. Lorin Woolley declared: "To be the head of a Dispensation, 7 wives [are] necessary. [To be the head of] the Patriarchal Order must have 5 wives. [To be] President of the Church - 3 wives [are necessary]."[15] Warren Jeffs is said to have more than seventy wives, and it is known that he married several of his father's (Rulon Jeffs) wives shortly after his father's death in 2002. The Allreds, LeBarons, Kingstons, and essentially all fundamentalists seem to hold true to this notion.

In contrast, Church leaders have never taught that a man gains an eternal advantage by acquiring as many wives as possible. During the period when polygamy was commanded (1852 to 1890), full compliance occurred when a man took a second wife. Marrying a third or fourth wife was not necessary.[16] In a letter to a Mormon bishop dated May 22, 1888, President Wilford Woodruff explained: "You ask some other questions con-

15. Quoted in Joseph White Musser, "Book of Remembrance," 21, n.d., holograph, photocopy in author's possession; see also *Items from a Book of Remembrance of Joseph W. Musser* (N.p.: published privately, n.d.), 16. See also Moroni Jessop, *Testimony of Moroni Jessop* (N.p.: published privately, n.d.), 2, photocopy in author's possession. Wives are said to become jewels in the crowns of their husbands.
16. D&C 132:19 promises godhood, exaltation, and a "continuation of the seeds" when "a man marries a wife" (monogamously), and they live worthily.

cerning how many living wives a man must have to fulfill the law. When a man, according to the revelation, married a wife under the holy order which God has revealed and then married another in the same way… so far as he has gone he has obeyed the law. I know of no requirement which makes it necessary for a man to have three living wives at a time."[17]

When Joseph C. Kingsbury was asked if Joseph Smith taught him "that a man could not be exalted in the hereafter unless he had more wives than one," Kingsbury replied: "No sir. He did not teach me that. He did not say anything about that."[18] Kingsbury also recalled: "I heard it preached from the stand that a man could be exalted in eternity with one wife."[19] Similarly, when Brigham Young was asked: "How general is polygamy among you?" He responded: "I could not say. Some of those present (heads of the Church) have each but one wife; others have more. Each determines what is his individual duty."[20]

It appears that the commandment to practice plural marriage between 1852 and 1890 was a singular directive given at a unique time and place with blessings attached. Accordingly, God's blessings flowed from obedience, not as some magical benefit from the practice of polygamy. Even during the 1852 to 1890 period, Church leaders did not encourage men to accumulate wives and offspring as they might amass wealth or property in the interest of some eternal advantage.

17. President Wilford Woodruff to Samuel Amos Woolley, fourth Bishop of the Ninth Ward, Salt Lake City, May 22, 1888, copy of typescript in author's possession.
18. Joseph Kingsbury, Testimony at the Temple Lot Case, part 2, page 225, questions 1028–29.
19. Joseph Kingsbury, Testimony at the Temple Lot Case, part 2, page 205, question 600.
20. Horace Greeley, *An Overland Journey from New York to San Francisco in the Summer of 1859* (1860; reprint New York: Ballantine Books, 1963), 138.

4. Mormon fundamentalists marry teenagers and have families with females as young as fourteen. Did early Church leaders and members follow this practice?

It is true that Joseph Smith and other early Church leaders were sealed to women as young as fourteen. However, historical evidence demonstrates that sexual relations were not a part of the relationships until the women were older. Eugene E. Campbell described Brigham Young's standard, which undoubtedly began in Nauvoo, regarding young plural brides:

> One of the more distressing developments was the number of men asking Young for permission to marry girls too young to bear children. To one man at Fort Supply, Young explained, "I don't object to your taking sisters named in your letter to wife if they are not too young and their parents and your president and all connected are satisfied, but I do not want children to be married to men before an age which their mothers can generally best determine." Writing to another man in Spanish Fork, he said, "Go ahead and marry them, but leave the children to grow." A third man in Alpine City was instructed, "It is your privilege to take more wives, but set a good example to the people, and leave the children long enough with their parents to get their growth, strength and maturity." To Louis Robinson, head of the church at Fort Bridger, Young advised, "Take good women, but let the children grow, then they will be able to bear children after a few years without injury." Another man in Santa Clara was told that it would be wise to marry an Indian girl but only if she were mature.[21]

Perhaps President Young's counsel is why one study showed that the average age for plural wives married in one

---

21. Eugene E. Campbell, *Establishing Zion: The Mormon Church in the American West 1847–1869* (Salt Lake City: Signature Books, 1988), 198 n. 5.

area of Utah during the nineteenth century was around twenty.[22]

Future President of the Church Wilford Woodruff married a fifteen-year-old named Emma Smith on November 11, 1843. Concerning that marriage, historian Thomas G. Alexander surmised: "He probably refrained from sexual relations with Emma until she became older, since she did not bear her first child, Hyrum Smith Woodruff, until October 4, 1857, seven months after she turned nineteen."[23]

Similarly, another apostle, Lorenzo Snow, waited until his future wife was older, rather than marrying here her at age fourteen.

> While the Houtz family were still living in Nauvoo, on a Sunday, Elenor and her parents were leaving church when Lorenzo Snow joined them. As they walked along, Lorenzo asked Elenor if she would promise to one day become his wife. Though, at the time, she was only fourteen she did make that promise. It has been erroneously written that she married at fourteen but church records and a letter written by Elenor to her Uncle Jacob Houtz, state her marriage date as 19 January 1848 [when she was eighteen]. She was married at Mt Pisgah by Brigham Young.[24]

It is significant that the Nauvoo City Council passed an ordinance on February 17, 1842, *raising* the minimum ages for marriage: "All male persons over the age of seventeen years, and females over the age of fourteen years, may contract and be

---

22. Larry Logue, "A Time of Marriage: Mormon Monogamy and Polygamy in a Utah Town," *Journal of Mormon History* 11 (1984): 6, 13.
23. Thomas G Alexander, *Things in Heaven and Earth: The Life and Times of Wilford Woodruff, a Mormon Prophet* (Salt Lake City: Signature Books, 1991), 168.
24. Glenn and Mildred H. Bray, "Elenor Houtz Snow," biographical sketch typescript, 2–3, LDS Church Archives, The Church of Jesus Christ of Latter-day Saints, Salt Lake City.

joined in marriage, provided, in all cases where either party is a minor, the consent of parents or guardians be first had."[25] Attorney Melina McTigue observed that concerning the cultural norms of that era: "Early English law set the age of consent at ten, the age was gradually raised over the years. In the nineteenth century, most states had set the age of consent at ten. A few states began by using twelve as the cutoff; Delaware set the age of consent at seven."[26]

The Mormon fundamentalist practice of marrying and having children by young teenagers greatly contrasts the practice of early Church pluralists, who were counseled to wait until their younger wives had matured before initiating physical relations that could result in pregnancy.

5. Mormon fundamentalists believe section 132 of the Doctrine and Covenants is strictly about polygamy. Is that true?

Mormon fundamentalists often assert that all of section 132 of the Doctrine and Covenants refers to plural marriage, including the statement: "all those who have this law revealed unto them must obey the same . . . if ye abide not that covenant, then are ye damned." (D&C 132:3–4). This interpretation is problematic. It is true that section 132 was given to Joseph Smith when he asked the Lord specifically about polygamy. Verses one and two state:

> Verily, thus saith the Lord unto you my servant Joseph, that inasmuch as you have inquired of my hand to know and understand wherein I, the Lord, justified my servants Abraham, Isaac, and Jacob, as also Moses, David and Solomon, my servants, as touching the principle and doctrine of their having many wives and

25. "Nauvoo Records," section one, Church Archives.
26. Melina McTigue, "Statutory Rape Law Reform in Nineteenth Century Maryland: An Analysis of Theory and Practical Change," (2002), http://www.law.georgetown.edu/glh/mctigue.htm.

concubines—Behold, and low, I am the Lord thy God,
and will answer thee as touching this matter.

Modern polygamists sometimes assume everything that follows Joseph's question (in verse one) deals strictly with polygamy, however, an examination of the remaining section shows that plural marriage itself is not mentioned until verse thirty-four.

Church scholars assert that the intervening verses actually discuss something much broader than polygamy; specifically, they introduce the law of eternal marriage or the law of celestial marriage and the new and everlasting covenant of marriage (which encompass the principle of plural marriage but is not limited to it). LDS theology holds that whenever this law and covenant are restored to earth and made available to a person, it must be accepted or damnation will result because there will be *no second chances* in the spirit world to comply and receive full blessings. Verses nineteen and twenty explain that compliance occurs whenever "a man" marries "a wife" by proper authority, and they live worthily. To that couple, the blessings of godhood are offered, and there is no mention of polygamy.

Latter-day Saints believe that Joseph Smith's specific question about plural marriage brought forth a much more comprehensive answer that dealt, not only with polygamy, but with the general laws and covenants governing marriages in eternity. In 1833, Joseph Smith received the same kind of answer to a different question. He prayed to know if tobacco use was appropriate during Church meetings.[27] In response, he was given section 89 of the Doctrine and Covenants, which contains a general health code for all Church members and is commonly referred to as the "Word of Wisdom." Joseph's specific prayer

---

27. See Brigham Young, in *Journal of Discourses,* 12:157–58, February 8, 1868.

about tobacco elicited a broad answer regarding many health issues including tobacco use.

Question	God's Answer	Scope of Answer
What about tobacco use?	Word of Wisdom (D&C 89)	A general health code that addresses tobacco use but is not limited strictly to it
What about polygamy?	The New and Everlasting Covenant of Marriage (D&C 132)	God's law of eternal marriage that includes plural marriage but is not limited strictly to it

6. Mormon fundamentalists believe that God's directive to "Go... and do the works of Abraham" in section 132:32 is a specific command to practice plural marriage. Is that true?

Some Mormon fundamentalists interpret D&C 132:32–33 as a command from God to practice plural marriage: "Go ye, therefore, and do the works of Abraham; enter ye into my law and ye shall be saved. But if ye enter not into my law ye cannot receive the promise of my Father, which he made unto Abraham."

In fact, Abraham did many good "works." He sought for the priesthood (Abr. 1:2–3), he presided righteously over his family, he paid his tithing (Alma 13:15), he kept his covenants, he received revelation, he was married by proper authority (D&C 132:37), he practiced polygamy, and, significantly, he offered up burnt offerings (Gen. 22:13). Latter-day Saints recognize that God has commanded them today to "do the works of Abraham" (D&C 132:32), but acknowledge that He has not authorized or commanded them to do all of Abraham's works. Specifically, Church members are not expected or permitted to offer up burnt offerings. Equally, they believe that God has also withdrawn His authorization and command to practice plural marriage. However, these limitations do not remove the divine directive for believers to emulate Abraham's other good works.

Importantly, Abraham "received" his wives; they were "given" to him (D&C 132:29, 37; see also 38–39) by the Lord through His authorized servants. Marriages performed without the authorization of the "one" man are freelance plural marriages and freelance polygamy is not doing the "works of Abraham." It seems that the Lord anticipated freelance plural marriages when He revealed D&C 132:18. "If a man marry a wife, and make a covenant with her for time and for all eternity, if that covenant not... through him whom I have anointed and appointed unto this power, then it is not valid neither of force when they are out of the world." In this verse God reveals that tradition, sincerity, personal revelation, and/or correct language cannot compensate for the lack of proper authorization.

Unauthorized priesthood ordinations are "dead works" in the eyes of the Lord (D&C 22:3). Twice in section 132, God emphasizes that His house is a "house of order" (D&C 132:8, 18), suggesting that order is important in establishing the validity of an eternal marriage. The Prophet Joseph plainly instructed: "All the ordinances, systems, and administrations on the earth are of no use to the children of men, unless they are ordained and authorized of God; for nothing will save a man but a legal administrator; for none others will be acknowledged either by God or angels."[28] "Doing the works of Abraham" requires a legal administrator to seal any and all eternal marriages, because that is the way Abraham did his own work.

---

28. Joseph Fielding Smith, comp. *Teachings of the Prophet Joseph Smith* (Salt Lake City: Deseret Book, 1976), 274.

7. What priesthood authority to Mormon fundamentalists claim to exercise when performing their marriages?

Doctrine and Covenants 132:18 states that any plural marriage that is not authorized by the "one" man holding the keys of sealing "is not valid neither of force when they are out of the world..." Early Church leaders solemnized plural unions using the priesthood keys held by the senior apostle, who rises to that position through seniority based on the date of his ordination as a member of the Quorum of the Twelve Apostles within the Church. Presidents of the LDS Church claim an orderly succession of sealing authority from Joseph Smith to Thomas S. Monson through the office of President, who has always been the senior apostle.

As discussed in the text below, Mormon fundamentalists have always used different authority or no authority at all. Many claim a line of authority leading back to Joseph Smith, but it comes through unheard of offices like "High Priest Apostles" and the "Right of the Firstborn" or through unheard of councils like the Council of Seven Friends (or Priesthood Council). Examining their claims reveals that the law of witnesses (2 Cor. 13:; D&C 6:28) was not followed by leaders such as Lorin C. Woolley, A. Dayer LeBaron, Elden Kingston, and others.

A few fundamentalist authorities claim the endowment of a new dispensation of authority directly from heaven. However, Joseph Smith was told he was bringing in the last dispensation (D&C 27:13).

Some fundamentalists believe that simply living a polygamous lifestyle is sufficient to garner God's blessings without worrying about authority issues. This sentiment was not shared by early priesthood leaders. In 1847, W. W. Phelps married three wives without Brigham Young's authorization. Although Phelps had clearly embraced a polygamous lifestyle, Young excommunicated him because his marriages were not performed by proper authority, telling him he had committed adultery.[29] At no time in this earth's history has freelance polygamy been viewed as eternally valuable.[30]

8. Concerning the Adam-God theory, what is more fundamental: the teachings of Joseph Smith and the scriptures regarding the identity of Adam, or ideas that were never fully explained that came afterwards?

Throughout the standard works and all of the teachings of Joseph Smith, the identity of Adam is consistently portrayed. He was a spirit son of God, our Heavenly Father, and he came to earth to endure a probationary period, relying on Jesus Christ's atonement. Moses 6:50–52, scripture received through Joseph Smith, teaches this clearly:

> God hath made known unto our fathers that all men must repent.
>
> And he called upon our father Adam by his own voice, saying: I am God; I made the world, and men before they were in the flesh.
>
> And he also said unto him: If thou wilt turn unto me, and hearken unto my voice, and believe, and repent of all thy transgressions, and be baptized, even in water, in the name of mine Only Begotten Son, who is full of grace and truth, which is Jesus Christ, the only name which shall be given under heaven, whereby salvation shall come unto the children of men, ye shall receive the gift of the Holy Ghost, asking all things in his name, and whatsoever ye shall ask, it shall be given you.

29. Richard Van Wagoner and Steven C. Walker, "The Joseph/Hyrum Smith Funeral Sermon, *BYU Studies* 23, no. 1 (1983): 6.
30. D&C 132:13, 15, and 18 explain that marriages, whether monogamist or polygamist, that are performed *without* proper authority end at death. Eternal marriage requires authorization through the "one" man who holds the sealing keys (see D&C 132:19–20, 39).

In 1852, President Brigham Young stated that Adam "is our Father and our God, and the only God with whom we have to do."[31] During his presidency, President Young made a few similar comments that, if transcribed correctly, seemed to contrast the traditional view. It appears that President Young never explained to his listeners how his views related to his own orthodox teachings on the topic, to the scriptures, or to the instructions of Joseph Smith, regarding the first man. Nor did he ever devote an entire discourse to the subject. Of the 1,500 known discourses of Brigham Young, a few dozen provides hints regarding his belief in the identity of Adam. Some of Brigham's teachings declared plain orthodox instructions about Adam:

> We believe in God the Father and in Jesus Christ our elder brother. We believe that God is a person of tabernacle, possessing in an infinitely higher degree all the perfections and qualifications of his mortal children. We believe that he made Adam after his own image and likeness, as Moses testifies.[32]
>
> I want to tell you, each and every one of you, that you are well acquainted with God our heavenly Father, or the great Eloheim. You are all well acquainted with Him, for there is not a soul of you but what has lived in His house and dwelt with Him year after year; and yet you are seeking to become acquainted with Him, when the fact is, you have merely forgotten what you did know. There is not a person here to-day but what is a son or a daughter of that Being. In the spirit world their spirits were first begotten and brought forth, and they lived there with their parents for ages before they came here. This, perhaps, is hard for many to believe, but it is the greatest nonsense in the world not to believe it. If you do not believe it, cease to call Him Father; and when you pray, pray to some other character.[33]

31. Brigham Young, in *Journal of Discourses,* 1:50–51, April 9, 1852.
32. Brigham Young, in *Journal of Discourses,* 10:230–31, July 8, 1863.
33. Brigham Young, in *Journal of Discourses,* 4:216, February 8, 1857.

> The world may in vain ask the question, "Who are we?" But the Gospel tells us that we are the sons and daughters of that God whom we serve. Some say, "We are the children of Adam and Eve." So we are, and they are the children of our Heavenly Father. We are all the children of Adam and Eve, and they and we are the offspring of Him who dwells in the heavens, the highest Intelligence that dwells anywhere that we have any knowledge of.[34]

In many ways, understanding the identity of Adam is like putting together a jigsaw puzzle. The standard works, accompanied by the teachings of Joseph Smith (and *some* of discourses of Brigham Young), give us many pieces that seem to fit snugly together, providing us with the traditional representation of the identity of Adam. However, if Brigham Young was quoted correctly, it appears that on a few occasions, he provided other puzzle pieces that currently are not easily accommodated, neither their interlocking edges, nor as a part of the overall panorama that restored gospel principles creates.

It may be that the puzzle pieces from President Brigham Young were corrupted through faulty transcription. Perhaps they indeed fit the puzzle in some unobvious way. Maybe the picture is three-dimensional, and we just do not know it yet. A few Church scholars have suggested that "Michael-Adam" may be the name of both God the Father and the first mortal man mentioned in the Bible. They posit that Brigham Young was just flip-flopping between the two beings, but his scribes were unclear in making the transitions, creating puzzle pieces of erroneous shapes.

Regardless, Adam-God theorists seem comfortable ripping out the scripture-based components and forcefully introducing new puzzle pieces, which are a composite of their own ideas and interpretations of Brigham's reported comments. Conse-

---

34. Brigham Young, in *Journal of Discourses,* 13:311–12, April 17, 1870.

quently, their Adam-God theory puzzles contain huge gaps, as many doctrinal pieces (from Joseph Smith and the scriptures) are forced out of the picture altogether. Furthermore, a review of Mormon fundamentalist interpretations demonstrates that they don't agree among themselves regarding important details Brigham failed to elucidate, creating a variety of distinct Adam-God theory puzzle artwork.

To believe that Brigham Young taught the Adam-God theory as promoted by Mormon fundamentalists is to believe that he freely contradicted Joseph Smith, John Taylor, the scriptures and, importantly, himself regarding the identity of Adam. This is untenable. Most likely, we have incomplete information regarding his intended instructions and/or the overall identity of God.

Until more information is revealed, it seems wise to patiently wait. Knowledge of the specific name of God the Father does not change the way we worship or our hopes for exaltation. Patience in understanding the "mystery of godliness" (1 Tim. 3:16; D&C 19:10) will be rewarded. We are promised that "the day shall come when you shall comprehend even God, being quickened in him and by him" (D&C 88:49) and that at a future time "nothing shall be withheld, whether there be one God or many gods, they shall be manifest. All thrones and dominions, principalities and powers, shall be revealed and set forth" (D&C 121:28–29).

9. Does God expect us to live the law of consecration now?

Mormon fundamentalists often place great emphasis upon the united order. However, Joseph Smith made no effort to implement the law of consecration in Nauvoo (see D&C 105:34), and Brigham Young waited until 1868, twenty-one years after arriving in Utah, to actively promote it. John Taylor ceased emphasizing it shortly after Brigham Young's death. It seems that early priesthood leaders felt little compulsion to put the law of consecration into operation, despite numerous opportunities to do so.

Importantly, most of the efforts of Mormon fundamentalists to live the actual law of consecration bear little resemblance. The scriptures plainly outline that this is a privilege (D&C 51:15). Doctrine & Covenants 42:31–34 specifies that the receiver of consecrated properties must be an authorized "bishop" of the Church, further demonstrating that the Lord would not find a freelance movement acceptable.

10. Some Mormon fundamentalist leaders exercise immense control over property, homes, marriages, and families of their followers. Did Joseph Smith, Brigham Young, John Taylor, and other Church leaders behave that way?

Today, Warren Jeffs, the Kingstons, and the leaders of several fundamentalist groups exert control over the marriages that occur among their followers. This contrasts Brigham Young's 1853 counsel: "I am free, and so are you. My advice to the sisters is, 'Never be sealed to any man unless you wish to be.' I say to you High Priests and Elders, 'Never from this time ask a woman to be sealed to you, unless she wants to be; but let the widows and children alone.'"[35] Controlling marriages was never a practice of early priesthood leaders. Individual free agency has been the rule and guide.

Through entities like the United Effort Plan or the Davis County Cooperative Society, Mormon fundamentalist leaders also exercise tight control over property and residences and call it "the law of consecration." But in reality, they are quite different.

In the law of consecration, properties are consecrated to the Church with the bishop acting as agent for the Church (D&C

35. Brigham Young, in *Journal of Discourses*, 6:307, April 8, 1853.

42:31–34; 51:12). Then after "testimonies" (i.e., discussions and interviews) between the member and the bishop, a decision is made regarding what is needed for the member's stewardship. That portion is then deeded back to the member; he is the owner (D&C 42:32). Members receive their own property and resources and then are left to utilize their own free agency to make choices that will bring prosperity or problems. No dominion, compulsion, or control (D&C 121:37) is exerted by bishops and high councils (or other priesthood leaders) who serve to administer to the poor using the resources from the bishop's storehouse (D&C 42:34; 51:13).

In contrast, the Kingston's Davis County Cooperative Society, the Allred united order communities in Montana and elsewhere, and the FLDS United Effort Plan (UEP) have received numerous consecrations of money, property, and other valuables from followers who joined the respective plans. However, as a general rule they do not deed back to their members a portion, conveying it to them as their (the members') own property. Instead, they maintain tight control over the resources and, consequently, tight control over all members of the plan. The lack of free agency in these purported united order organizations greatly contrasts the teachings and practices of all early priesthood leaders.

11. *Some Mormon fundamentalists seem comfortable using deception to defraud the government of welfare subsidies. Have Church leaders ever encouraged men to marry plural wives they could not support?*

Much evidence exists to show that during the past few decades, many plural wives of Mormon fundamentalist men have deceived the government in order to obtain welfare assistance and medical coverage. The deception occurs as plural wives fail to identify the father of their children in official records as required by state laws; the mothers supply spurious names or say they do not know. Through this fraud, fathers are able to shift their responsibilities for the material support of their plural families to state welfare programs.

Being responsible for the temporal needs of the members of the UEP in the 1980s, Bishop Fred Jessop in Colorado City, Arizona, reportedly encouraged FLDS members in the area to take advantage of government assistance in the form of welfare and the WIC (woman-infant-child) programs. In 2003, thirty-three percent of the town's residents received food stamps—compared to the state average of 4.7 percent resulting in more than $6 million a year in public funds being funneled into the Community of Colorado City. Jon Krakauer, author of a controversial book on contemporary Mormon fundamentalism, wrote: "Fundamentalists call defrauding the government 'bleeding the beast' and regard it as a virtuous act."[36]

Welfare subsidies received by members of the Kingston clan resulted in the prosecution of Ortell Kingston by the state of Utah in 1983 for fraud. The case was settled with Kingston paying the state $250,000.

Independent polygamist Tom Green was charged with criminal non-support among other crimes. The state of Utah asserted that he and his "wives" had received more than $647,000 in state and federal assistance, including $203,000 in food stamps and nearly $300,000 in medical and dental expenses since 1985. After a drawn out trial process, he was convicted and sentenced to prison.

In 1993, one Utah State Department of Social Services

---

36. Jon Krakauer, *Under the Banner of Heaven: A Story of Violent Faith* (New York: Doubleday, 2003), 13. See also Rena Chynoweth with Dean M. Shapiro, *The Blood Covenant* (Austin, Tex.: Diamond Books, 1990), 46–47; Melissa Merrill (pseud.), *Polygamist's Wife* (Salt Lake City: Olympus Publishing, 1975), 64; Kathryn M. Daynes, *More Wives Than One: Transformation of the Mormon Marriage System 1840–1910* (Urbana: University of Illinois, 2001), 210–11.

employee estimated that through her office, "300 polygamous families receive from between $500 and $1600 worth of food stamps each month for families with an average of 15 members." She further explained: "The attitude of some polygamists is 'the government is untrustworthy and corrupt, and I'm above it—but give me those food stamps and free medical care.'"[37]

In contrast, the apostle Paul set the standard incumbent upon God's followers: "But if any provide not for his own, and specially for those of his own house, he hath denied the faith, and is worse than an infidel" (1 Tim. 5:8). Doctrine and Covenants 83:2 and 4, explain: "Women have claim on their husbands for their maintenance... All children have claim upon their parents for their maintenance until they are of age." At no time have Church authorities encouraged men to marry wives they could not provide for or support materially.

12. Mormon fundamentalists do no missionary work. Is it possible that God would exempt any of His followers from this fundamental responsibility?

It appears that Mormon fundamentalist leaders seldom, if ever, send out missionaries to preach the gospel and to baptize. If LDS Church members were to join a fundamentalist faction, they would instantly be released as member-missionaries. Why? Because their new fundamentalist leaders would not expect them to perform missionary work.

Doctrine and Covenants 84:75–76 states: "The gospel is unto all who have not received it. But, verily I say unto all *those to whom the kingdom has been given—from you it must be preached unto them*" (italics mine). Mormon fundamentalists usually claim to represent the "kingdom of God" on earth and to possess all priesthood keys (including the "keys of the gathering of

Israel" mentioned in D&C 110:11; 35:25). Yet they do not claim to have received all priesthood responsibilities that Joseph Smith, Brigham Young, and other early leaders shouldered. One of the foremost responsibilities is the need to do missionary work (see D&C 1:4,18; 4:3; 18:10–16; 33:6–10; 60:2–3; 68:8; etc.).

Anciently, Enoch, Noah, Abraham, and other of God's prophets served as missionaries and sent missionaries. It appears that no individual or group of God's followers in the history of the world who received the gospel was exempted from this important duty. The one exception, according to their own theology, is the Mormon fundamentalists.

It seems that one function of the Holy Spirit is to inspire receptive listeners to share the gospel. Doctrine and Covenants 14:8 specifies:

> And it shall come to pass, that if you shall ask the Father in my name, in faith believing, you shall receive the Holy Ghost, which giveth utterance, that you may stand as a witness of the things of which you shall both hear and see, and also that you may declare repentance unto this generation.

For example, after their conversion, the four sons of Mosiah felt "desirous that salvation should be declared to every creature, for they could not bear that any human soul should perish; yea, even the very thoughts that any soul should endure endless torment did cause them to quake and tremble. And thus did the Spirit of the Lord work upon them" (Mosiah 28:3–4). Similarly, Enos cried unto the Lord in "mighty prayer" for many hours until he received a remission of his sins. He immediately "began to feel a desire for the welfare of my brethren, the Nephites; wherefore, I did pour out my whole soul unto God for them" (Enos 1:9). After being assured on their behalf, he also prayed "with many long strugglings for my brethren, the Lamanites" (Enos 1:11).

Having read thousands of pages of religious discourses and other writings produced over the past century by both Mormon fundamentalist leaders and LDS Church leaders, I have noticed the striking lack of concern on the part of fundamentalists for missionary work. From the 1920s to the present, they usually see themselves as a privileged group who, unlike nineteenth-century LDS polygamists, do not need to serve as missionaries to gather scattered Israel.

Leroy S. Johnson, FLDS leader from 1952 to 1986, manifested this elitist mentality: "Let us look to our own selves. If we labor from now on and save no one but our own souls, how great will our joy be in the Kingdom of God."[38] This self-focused attitude sharply contrasts the Church's beliefs as portrayed in D&C 18:14–15: "Wherefore, you are called to cry repentance unto this people. And if it so be that you should labor all your days in crying repentance unto this people, and bring, save it be one soul unto me, how great shall be your joy with him in the kingdom of my Father!"

A spirit exists within the fundamentalist movement that moves its adherents. It moves them to tears; it gives them undeniable emotional feelings; it moves them to practice plural marriage; but, ironically, it does not move them to share the "good news" with those who have not received it. This distinction exemplifies perhaps the most important difference between the spirit of Mormon fundamentalism and the Spirit that guided Joseph Smith, Brigham Young, John Taylor, and other early Church members. The Spirit they followed prompted them to be polygamists *and* missionaries. Today that Spirit prompts Latter-day Saints to embrace eternal marriage and to continue missionary efforts.

---

38. Leroy S. Johnson, *The L. S. Johnson Sermons*, 7 vols. (Hildale, Utah: Twin Cities Courier, 1983–84), 5:58.

13. Historically, Mormon fundamentalists have done little or no temple work to save the dead. Is it possible that they are exempted from this important work?

The man who holds the keys of sealing also carries the responsibility to oversee saving ordinance work for the dead. "For him to whom these keys are given there is no difficulty in obtaining a knowledge of facts in relation to the salvation of the children of men, both as well for the dead as for the living" (D&C 128:11).

Joseph Smith wrote: "And now my dearly beloved brethren and sisters, let me assure you that these are principles in relation to the dead and the living that cannot be lightly passed over, as pertaining to our salvation. For their salvation is necessary and essential to our salvation, as Paul says concerning the fathers—that they without us cannot be made perfect—neither can we without our dead be made perfect" (D&C 128:15).

The Prophet Joseph also instructed: "How are they to become saviors on Mount Zion? By building their temples, erecting their baptismal fonts, and going forth and receiving all the ordinances, baptisms, confirmations, washings, anointings, ordinations and sealing powers upon their heads, in behalf of all their progenitors who are dead, and redeem them that they may come forth in the first resurrection and be exalted to thrones of glory with them; and herein is the chain that binds the hearts of the fathers to the children, and the children to the fathers, which fulfills the mission of Elijah."[39]

Despite this clear emphasis from Joseph Smith, current research suggests that for several decades between 1930 and 1980, fundamentalist leaders never used their alleged priesthood keys to perform saving ordinance work for the dead. In their teachings and practices, fundamentalist leaders have consistently treated proxy work as a non-issue.

---

39. Smith , *Teachings of the Prophet Joseph Smith,* 330.

Mormon Fundamentalism and the Restoration of Plural Marriage

During the past eighty years, members of The Church of Jesus Christ of Latter-day Saints have been increasingly exposed to the activities of "Mormon fundamentalists" as portrayed in the media. Issues surrounding the continued practice of polygamy usually bring fundamentalism to the forefront, but Church members may wonder about other differences. They may puzzle over the allegations that their Church and religion have lost *fundamental* principles that are reportedly being perpetuated by dissenters. If something is currently missing from the doctrines and practices of the Church, members want to know what it is and why it was jettisoned. And if the accusations are false, there is desire to comprehend the deceptions and the forces that have otherwise empowered the so-called "fundamentalist" movement.

RELIGIOUS "FUNDAMENTALISTS"

The term "fundamentalist" was first used to describe a group of activist Protestant Christians in the 1920s to depict a "person willing to do battle royal for fundamentals of the faith."[40] The first time the title was applied in the "Mormon" arena was by Joseph Musser who used it to describe himself and his followers in 1935.[41]

---

40. Nancy T. Ammerman, "North American Protestant Fundamentalism," in Martin E. Marty and R. Scott Appleby, eds., *Fundamentalisms Observed* (Chicago: University of Chicago Press, 1991), 2.
41. Joseph White Musser, "The Short Creek Embroglio," *Truth* 1 (October 1935): 52.

Richard T. Antoun, author of *Understanding Fundamentalisms*, explained: "The movement, like the word fundamentalism, initially emerged among rural and urban Presbyterians and Baptists in the early decades of the twentieth century."[42] "All fundamentalists are generally viewed as doctrinaire followers of sacred scripture, dwellers in and on the past, and naive simplifiers of complex world events involved in a struggle between good and evil."[43]

The development of fundamentalist groups has affected every major religion on earth, including the formation of Catholic fundamentalists, Christian fundamentalists, Islamic fundamentalists, Jewish fundamentalists, and even "fundamentalists" among the fundamentalist factions. Within the realm of the restored gospel, dissenters who continued to practice plural marriage after 1904 eventually adopted the title of "Mormon Fundamentalists."

In order to understand the genesis of Mormon fundamentalism, a knowledge of the history of plural marriage is required. Fundamentalists of all persuasions are reactionists. They react to changes in the mother church, changes they believe are harmful or unauthorized. The discontinuation of plural marriage by The Church of Jesus Christ of Latter-day Saints in 1904 was the primary triggering event that eventually guided dozens, and then hundreds and thousands, of nonconformists to leave the confines of the Church to form their own religious organizations.

---

42. Richard T. Antoun, as quoted in Bruce Lawrence, *Defenders of God: The Fundamentalist Revolt against the Modern Age* (Columbia: University of South Carolina Press, 1989), 230.
43. Richard T. Atoun, *Understanding Fundamentalism: Christian Islamic, and Jewish Movements* (Walnut Creek, Calif.: Altamira Press, 2001), 1–2.

JOSEPH SMITH RESTORES
THE PRACTICE OF PLURAL MARRIAGE

Of all the gospel principles restored through the Prophet Joseph Smith, plural marriage was perhaps the most novel. While serving as an apostle, Gordon B. Hinckley wrote: "Mormonism claims to be a restoration of God's work in all previous dispensations. The Old Testament teaches that the patriarchs—those men favored of God in ancient times—had more than one wife under divine sanction. In the course of the development of the Church in the nineteenth century, it was revealed to the leader of the Church that such a practice of marriage again should be entered into."[44]

Precisely when Joseph Smith learned of the correctness of plural marriage is not known. He translated the Book of Mormon in 1830, which states: "For there shall not any man among you have save it be one wife; and concubines he shall have none. . . . For if I will, saith the Lord of Hosts, raise up seed unto me, I will command my people; otherwise they shall hearken unto these things" (Jacob 2:27, 30). While specifying monogamy, this statement leaves the door open for future polygamy should God see fit to allow it.

It appears that sometime shortly after the Book of Mormon was published, Joseph Smith learned that plural marriage was a true doctrine and would eventually be practiced by Church members. In 1831, Joseph revised the Bible noting the accounts of the ancient patriarchs who practiced polygamy. Abraham was married to Sarai (Sarah), Hagar (Gen. 16: 1–3), and concubines (Gen. 25:6).

Joseph Smith, Jr.

44. Gordon B. Hinckley, *Teachings of Gordon B. Hinckley* (Salt Lake City: Deseret Book, 1997), 457.

Jacob (renamed Israel by God) had twelve sons by four wives. Moses too was a polygamist (Ex. 2:21 and Num. 12:1). Early Church member Lyman E. Johnson recalled that "Joseph had made known to him as early as 1831 that plural marriage was a correct principle."[45]

Evidence suggests that Joseph Smith attempted one plural marriage during the 1830s, to Fanny Alger in 1835-36. However, it wasn't until the early 1840s that the Prophet would try again. Joseph B. Noble claimed that he was first introduced to the subject by Joseph in the fall of 1840, when the Prophet asked him to perform the first plural sealing in Nauvoo the next year. Between 1841 and 1844, Joseph Smith married additional wives and authorized others to do so.[46]

THE KEYS OF SEALING RESTORED

In conjunction with the reestablishment of plural marriage was the restoration of sealing authority, allowing Joseph to "bind on earth" things that will be "bound in heaven" including marriages (Matt. 16:19). During the dedication of the Kirtland Temple on April 3, 1836, Joseph and Oliver Cowdery received a visitation from Jesus Christ and later Elijah (D&C 110:2, 13–15). Elijah bestowed upon Joseph Smith the keys of sealing authority, allowing him to seal marriages that would endure beyond the grave and into the eternities. Eternal marriage and plural marriage are part of the new and everlasting covenant of marriage. Equally, the new and everlasting covenant of marriage is part of the new and everlasting covenant, which Joseph began restoring in 1830 (see D&C 22:1).

The Prophet wrote: "It may seem to some to be a very bold

---

45. As recalled by his mission companion, Orson Pratt, in *Millennial Star* 40 (December 16, 1874): 788.
46. See volume one of forthcoming publication by Brian C. Hales, *Joseph Smith's Polygamy* (Salt Lake City: Greg Kofford Books, 2009).

doctrine that we talk of—a power which records or binds on earth and binds in heaven. Nevertheless, in all ages of the world, whenever the Lord has given a dispensation of the priesthood to any man by actual revelation, or any set of men, this power has always been given. Hence, whatsoever those men did in authority, in the name of the Lord . . . it became a law on earth and in heaven, and could not be annulled, according to the decrees of the great Jehovah" (D&C 128:9).

Joseph Smith insisted that the sealing authority is tightly controlled by the key holder. An 1843 revelation clarified: "There is never but *one* on the earth at a time on whom this power and the keys of this priesthood are conferred. . . . Behold, mine house is a house of order, saith the Lord God, and not a house of confusion" (D&C 132:7–8; italics added). It also pointed out that even if the proper language is used and both individuals are sincere, marriages performed without proper authorization of the "one" are "not valid neither of force when they are out of the world" (D&C 132:18). In studying the claims of Mormon fundamentalists, the issue of priesthood keys cannot be over-emphasized.

According to D&C 132:7, 18, 19, the authority of the "one" man is absolutely necessary, in all cases, in all places throughout the world. The "one" man may commission other men with authority to seal, but they are always subject to the keys that he holds. "It is necessary to know who holds the keys of power, and who does not, or we may be likely to be deceived," taught Joseph Smith.[47] The "one" man regulates the sealing of both monogamist and polygamist marriages because both types of marriages utilize the very same keys. There are no specific keys of sealing for monogamist marriages and no separate set of sealing keys for plural marriages. Both types of marriages involve the very same authority. Plural marriage requires the repeated

---

47. Joseph Fielding Smith, comp., *Teachings of the Prophet Joseph Smith,* (Salt Lake City: Deseret Book, 1976), 336.

use of that authority, in each instance, sealing one woman to one man in eternal matrimony.

On one occasion, assosciate President of the Church Hyrum Smith proceeded to seal a couple without his brother's consent, Joseph being absent from Nauvoo at the time. Brigham Young later referred to this occasion saying that no one could "act on the sealing principle only as he was dictated by Joseph. This was proven, for Hyrum did undertake to seal without counsel."[48] When the Prophet returned and discovered what had occurred, he strongly cautioned Hyrum saying that if he ever did it again, "he would go to hell and all those he sealed with him."[49] Joseph annulled Hyrum's actions and later resealed the couple. LDS scholar, Andrew Ehat observed: "This early experience with regard to the authority to perform marriage sealings . . . illustrates the exclusive authority that Joseph Smith held: That certain of the presiding keys of the priesthood were not to be delegated."[50]

Hyrum would later teach "No marriage is valid in the morn of the resurrection unless the marriage covenant be sealed on earth by one having the keys and power from Almighty God to seal on earth as it shall be bound in heaven."[51] In 1845, Brigham Young would further clarify: "Joseph said that the sealing power is always vested in one man, and that there never was, nor never would be but one man on the earth at a time to hold the keys of the sealing power in the Church. That all sealings must be performed by the man holding the keys or by his dictation, and that man is the President of the Church."[52]

48. Brigham Young to William Smith, August 9, 1845, Brigham Young Collection, Church Archives.

49. Andrew F. Ehat, "Joseph Smith's Introduction of Temple Ordinances and the Mormon Succession Question" (master's thesis, Brigham Young University, 1982), 71.

50. Ibid., 47–48.

51. Hyrum Smith, Discourse, April 8, 1844, in Minutes Collection, Church Archives.

52. Brigham Young to William Smith, August 9, 1845, Church Archives.

BRIGHAM YOUNG HOLDS
THE KEYS AFTER JOSEPH SMITH'S DEATH

The moment Brigham Young heard of Joseph Smith's June 27, 1844 death, he was in the East doing missionary work. "The first thing that I thought of was whether Joseph had taken the keys of the kingdom with him from the earth," Brigham remembered. "Brother Orson Pratt sat at my left; we were both leaning back in our chairs. Bringing my hand down on my knee, I said, 'the keys of the kingdom are right here with the church.'"[53] Benjamin F. Johnson recalled the meeting where the Prophet charged the apostles with bearing off the kingdom:

> At one of the last meetings... in the presence of the Quorum of the Twelve and others who were encircled around him, he arose, gave a review of his life and sufferings, and of the testimonies he had borne, and said that the Lord had now accepted his labors and sacrifices, and did not require him longer to carry the responsibilities and burden and bearing off of this kingdom, and turning to those around him, including the 12, he said, "And in the name of the Lord, Jesus Christ I now place it upon you my brethren of this council and I shake my skirts clear of all responsibility from this time forth."[54]

Brigham knew that he held the priesthood keys, along with the other members of the Quorum of the Twelve, and that he, as the senior apostle, presided. Brigham Young had been specially prepared by Joseph Smith to lead. Just a few months earlier, in January of that year, the Prophet instructed Brigham regarding the administration of the highest temple ordinances and then authorized him to administer them to other members of the quorum even though the Nauvoo Temple was not yet completed. Consequently, the Quorum of the Twelve was the

---

53. *Millennial Star* 26 (June 4, 1864): 359.
54. Benjamin F. Johnson, *My Life's Review* (Independence, Mo.: Zion's Printing and Publishing, 1947), 99.

only presiding priesthood quorum that had received all temple ordinances. Brigham explained: "No man can put another between the Twelve and the Prophet Joseph. Why? Because Joseph was their file leader and he has committed into their hands the keys of the Kingdom for all the world."[55] In 1848, President Young taught: "No man was ever ordained to any higher order than an Apostle – and that Joseph Smith never received any higher ordination."[56]

During the two years after the Prophet's death, the number of plural marriages expanded five-fold, involving up to 10

percent of all Latter-day Saints. Once the westward migration was well underway, most Church members were aware of the doctrine. In 1852, Brigham Young announced to the world that plural marriage was a doctrinal tenet of the Church and that Latter-day Saints were expected to obey it. Practicing it by proper authority was paramount. No freelance plural marriages were

Brigham Young

permitted. Joseph Smith had instructed: "All the ordinances, systems, and administrations on the earth are of no use to the children of men, unless they are ordained and authorized of God; for nothing will save a man but a legal administrator; for none others will be acknowledged either by God or angels."[57]

Brigham Young followed this council strictly. W. W. Phelps was sent on a mission in 1847. While serving in the eastern states, he married three wives polygamously. However,

55. Woodruff, *Wilford Woodruff's Journal: 1833–1898*, 2:437.
56. William Greenwood, Diary, October 8, 1848, as quoted in D. Michael Quinn, *The Mormon Hierarchy: Origins of Power* (Salt Lake City: Signature Books, 1997), 67.
57. Smith, *Teachings of the Prophet Joseph Smith*, 274.

Phelps's mission companion, Henry B. Jacobs, performed the marriages without having first obtained permission from President Young. Upon returning to Salt Lake City with the three women as new wives, Brigham Young heard the story. Hosea Stout, an attorney and police officer in Nauvoo and Winter Quarters, noted:

> Went to a council today which had been called to investigate the cases of H[enry]. B. Jacobs and W. N. Phelps [*sic*] while they were East on a mission.
>
> It appeared that Phelps had while East last summer got some new ideas into three young women and they had consented to become his wives and got Jacobs to marry them to him in St. Louis and he lived with them as such all the way to this place. After a long and tedious hearing of the matter which was altogether their own admissions, President Young decided that Phelps had committed adultery every time that he had laid with one of them.[58]

Phelps was excommunicated on December 6, 1847. This account demonstrates that even though W. W. Phelps was sincerely trying to follow Church teachings regarding polygamy, his plural marriages were unauthorized and therefore considered adulterous by Brigham Young.

During the first three decades of living in the Rocky Mountains, polygamous unions expanded as did the persecution from the federal government. President Young passed away on August 29, 1877, and a few weeks later in October general conference, John Taylor was sustained as President of the Quorum of the Twelve, the presiding apostle on earth. The next day he taught: "You voted yesterday that the Twelve should be Prophets, Seers, and Revelators . . . this is embraced in the Apostleship, which has been given by the Almighty, and which

58. Juanita Brooks, ed., *On the Mormon Frontier: The Diary of Hosea Stout, 1844–1861*, 2 vols. (Salt Lake City: University of Utah Press, 1964), 1:289.

embraces all the keys, powers and authorities ever conferred upon man."[59] President Taylor presided until his passing on July 25, 1887.

59. John Taylor, in *Journal of Discourses* 26 vols. (Liverpool: F. D. Richards, 1855–86), 19:125, October 7, 1877.

Wilford Woodruff
and the 1890 Manifesto

With the death of John Taylor, Wilford Woodruff became the "one" man holding the keys of sealing. He would face unique challenges, unknown to his predecessors, and his leadership decisions would transform the Church and its membership.

AS THE KEY HOLDER,
WILFORD WOODRUFF ISSUES THE MANIFESTO

The 1880s were a turbulent time with federal legislation passed in 1882 and 1889 against plural marriage. On May 19, 1890, the Supreme Court ruled that the government could rightfully dissolve the Corporation of The Church of Jesus Christ of Latter-day Saints and confiscate the Church's holdings, including the temples at Logan, Manti, and St. George and the Salt Lake Temple nearing completion, appropriating their value for charitable use.

President Woodruff could easily discern the disastrous effect this would have upon the Church and its mission. By dissolving the Church as a corporate entity and imprisoning practicing polygamists, Church leaders would lose the ability to do missionary work—to effectuate the final "gathering" of the elect. And with the loss of the temples,

Wilford Woodruff

the commandment given to the Latter-day Saints to accomplish temple ordinance work for the dead would be completely curtailed.

On the other hand, for several decades polygamy had been central to Latter-day Saint doctrine, identity and solidarity. At one time, up to 20 to 25 percent of LDS adults were members of polygamous households. The thought of suspending the practice brought poignant recollections of the sacrifices that Church members had suffered for the principle, including hundreds who had spent time in prison. Thousands more had been involved in hiding its practice, and, by 1890, over 12,000 Latter-day Saints in Utah had been prevented from voting. However, to ignore the momentum of governmental interference was not an agreeable option either.

On the morning of September 24, 1890, President Woodruff entered the First Presidency's office with new resolve. His journal entry for that date states: "I have arrived at a point in the history of the Church of Jesus Christ of Latter-day Saints when I am under the necessity of acting for the temporal salvation of the church."[60] He presented papers that he had written, which contained the text that would become the Manifesto:

> To Whom it may concern:
>
> Press dispatches having been sent for political purposes, from Salt Lake City, which have been widely published, to the effect that the Utah Commission, in their recent report to the Secretary of the Interior, allege that plural marriages are still being solemnized and that forty or more such marriages have been contracted in Utah since last June or during the past year, also that in public discourses the leaders of the Church have taught, encouraged and urged the continuance of the practice of polygamy—
>
> I, therefore, as President of the Church of Jesus

---

60. Woodruff, *Wilford Woodruff's Journal, 1833–1898*, September 25, 1890; spelling and punctuation standardized.

Christ of Latter-day Saints, do hereby, in the most solemn manner, declare that these charges are false. We are not teaching polygamy or plural marriage, nor permitting any person to enter into its practice, and I deny that either forty or any other number of plural marriages have during that period been solemnized in our Temples or in any other place in the Territory.

One case has been reported, in which the parties allege that the marriage was performed in the Endowment House, in Salt Lake City, in the Spring of 1889, but I have not been able to learn who performed the ceremony; whatever was done in this matter was without my knowledge. In consequence of this alleged occurrence the Endowment House was, by my instructions, taken down without delay.

Inasmuch as laws have been enacted by Congress forbidding plural marriages, which laws have been pronounced constitutional by the court of last resort, I hereby declare my intentions to submit to those laws, and to use my influence with the members of the Church over which I preside to have them do likewise.

There is nothing in my teachings to the Church or in those of my associates, during the time specified, which can be reasonably construed to inculcate or encourage polygamy; and when any Elder of the Church has used language which appeared to convey any such teaching, he has been promptly reproved. And I now publicly declare that my advice to the Latter-day Saints is to refrain from contracting any marriage forbidden by the law of the land.

Wilford Woodruff
President of the Church of Jesus Christ of Latter-day Saints

This manifesto was presented at general conference two weeks later. Then Wilford Woodruff spoke assuring the Saints that "the Lord will never permit me nor any other man who stands as the President of this Church, to lead you astray. It is not in the program. It is not in the mind of God. If I were to attempt that, the Lord would remove me out of my place, and so He will any other man who attempts to lead the children of men astray from the oracles of God and from their duty."[61] He was echoing Brigham Young who taught in 1862: "The Lord Almighty leads this Church, and he will never suffer you to be led astray if you are found doing your duty. You may go home and sleep as sweetly as a babe in its mother's arms, as to any danger of your leaders leading you astray, for if they should try to do so the Lord would quickly sweep them from the earth."[62]

First Counselor George Q. Cannon then explained that God had accepted the sacrifice of the Saints and removed the need to practice plural marriage:

> I know myself that it was the will of God that the Manifesto should be given. I know it was the will of God that the word should go to the Latter-day Saints that plural marriage should cease and that we should conform to the requirements of the law . . .
>
> God gave the command, and it required the command of God to cause us to change our attitude. President Woodruff holds the same authority that the man did through whom the revelation came to the Church. *It required the same authority to say to us, "It is enough." God has accepted of your sacrifice.* He has looked down upon you and seen what you have passed through, and how determined you were to keep His commandments, and now He says, *"It is enough." It is the same authority that gave us the principle.* It is not the word of man. Now, it is for us to obey the Law.[63]

---

61. Wilford Woodruff, in *Collected Discourses*, 2:137, October 6, 1890. .
62. Brigham Young, in *Journal of Discourses*, 9:289, February 23, 1862.
63. George Q. Cannon, "Remarks Given at Logan," *Deseret Weekly*, November 17, 1891, 6. See also *Deseret Evening News*, November 14, 1891, and *Collected Discourses*, 2:295. (Italics added.)

During the following year President Woodruff gave additional insights, teaching that the manifesto was from God, not man. He said: "He [God] has told me exactly what to do." "The God of heaven commanded me to do what I did do." "I wrote what the Lord told me to write." Later he would also teach: "Almighty God commanded me to do what I did."[64] "The Son of God felt disposed to have [the manifesto] presented to the Church."[65] "What I said to the people of our Church I said by inspiration, as I view it—by the mind and will of the Lord. I intended to give them to understand that we should stop the practice of plural marriage."[66] Privately Wilford Woodruff also stated "that the manifesto was just as authoritative and binding as though it had been given in the form of 'Thus saith the Lord.'"[67]

According to the teachings and actions of President Woodruff, the 1890 Manifesto removed the commandment to practice plural marriage from the Saints. However, it did not remove permission to do so. It appears that during his presidency, Second Counselor Joseph F. Smith received private permission to authorize plural marriages, independent of the Church President's specific case-by-case approval.

PLURAL MARRIAGES 1890–1904

Wilford Woodruff died on September 2, 1898, leaving Lorenzo Snow as the senior apostle and the "one" holding the keys of sealing. In conjunction with his new responsibil-

---

64. Stuy, *Collected Discourses*, 2:288–89.

65. From a discourse at the sixth session of the dedication of the Salt Lake Temple, April 1893. Typescript of Dedicatory Services, Church Archives. See also Official Declaration 1.

66. Wilford Woodruff, Testimony before the Master in Chancery, October 19–20, 1891, as published in the *Deseret Weekly*, October 23, 1891, 4–5.

67. First Presidency Office Journal, October 21, 1891, as found in D. Michael Quinn, "LDS Church Authority and New Plural Marriages, 1890–1904," *Dialogue: A Journal of Mormon Thought* 18 (Spring 1985): 51.

Lorenzo Snow

ity, President Snow related: "the Lord Jesus Christ appeared to me at the time of the death of President Woodruff. He instructed me to go right ahead and reorganize the First Presidency of the Church at once and not wait as had been done after the death of the previous presidents, and that I was to succeed President Woodruff."[68]

As President of the Church in 1899, Lorenzo Snow was openly adamant in his attempts to stop the secret polygamous sealings that were rumored to have occurred after 1890. He declared: "I will say now before this people, that the principle of plural marriage is not practiced. I have never, in one single instance, allowed any person to have that ceremony performed, and there are no such marriages at the present time, nor has [sic] there been during the time of my presidency over this church."[69]

With the deaths of George Q. Cannon on April 12, 1901, and President Lorenzo Snow six months later, Joseph F. Smith became the "one" man. As the senior apostle holding the keys of sealing, President Smith was initially more approachable than his two predecessors had been with regards to the performance of new secret plural marriages. Accordingly, between 1901 and April of 1904, over sixty plural marriages were authorized and performed. President Smith's relaxation with respect to new secret plural marriages soon generated a wave of rumors that were difficult to refute. Eventually, a whirlwind of national opposition blew into Church headquarters.

---

68. LeRoi C. Snow, "Remarkable Manifestation to Lorenzo Snow," *Church News,* April 2, 1938, 3, 8.
69. Eugene Young, "Revival of the Mormon Problem," *North American Review* 168 (April 1899): 484–85. In Quinn, "LDS Church Authority and New Plural Marriages," 69 and n. 240.

In March 1904, President Smith was called to Washington to testify in the Smoot hearings. There he was grilled by senators seeking to discover any duplicitous behavior with respect to new plural marriages. Within weeks of returning home, President Joseph F. Smith issued an "official statement" that has been called the "second manifesto." It was remarkably similar to the 1890 Manifesto, except that it promised "excommunication" to individuals who would not comply. It appears that Joseph F. Smith completely stopped prospective authorization of new plural marriages after that statement was issued. It was an official end to plural marriages that were officially sanctioned by the President of the Church.

Historian Jan Shipps observed that in 1890, the "Saints had to be converted away from polygamy. . . . Plural marriage was introduced to the Saints who, ever so slowly, converted to it in the early years and the Saints gave it up in a comparably slow process that often involved 'conversion' away from the practice. With remarkable symmetry, life was given to the practice and taken away from it."[70]

Joseph F. Smith

70. Jan Shipps, "The Principle Revoked: A Closer Look at the Demise of Plural Marriage," *Journal of Mormon History* 11 (1984): 76–77.

Plural Marriage Commanded, Permitted, and Not Permitted

As outlined above, God commanded the Latter-day Saints between 1852 and 1890 to practice plural marriage. Historical research also shows that the 1890 Manifesto did not stop the practice. It appears that Church Presidents Wilford Woodruff, Lorenzo Snow, and Joseph F. Smith continued to secretly authorize polygamous unions to be performed between 1890 and 1904. Most of those were performed in Mexico and Canada, but not all. Then, in 1904, President Joseph F. Smith issued the "official statement" heralding an end to future authorizations for plural marriages.

A review of the scriptures and LDS Church history shows

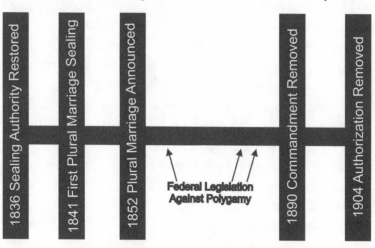

1836 Sealing Authority Restored

1841 First Plural Marriage Sealing

1852 Plural Marriage Announced

Federal Legislation Against Polygamy

1890 Commandment Removed

1904 Authorization Removed

History of Plural Marriage

that polygamy may rarely be *commanded* of the Lord's people. At other times, it may be *permitted,* and in many other times, it is *not permitted.* Latter-day Saints believe that it is all according to how the Lord "will command His people" (Jacob 2:30) and that it is regulated through the "one" man who holds the keys (D&C 132:7–8).

AT TIMES, PLURAL MARRIAGE IS *NOT PERMITTED*

It appears that at many times and places in earth's history, plural marriage was *not permitted* by God. LDS theology holds that during those periods, living righteously in eternal monogamous marriages brought full exaltation.

The Book of Mormon provides an example of a prophet and his family living righteously in monogamy. Lehi's son Jacob revealed that his father was personally commanded by God to be a monogamist. Decades after his father' death, while counseling the errant Nephites, Jacob referred to "the commandment of the Lord, which was given unto our father—that they should have save it were *one wife* and concubines they should have none" (Jacob 3:5; italics added). This commandment was given to Lehi before he arrived in America (the "promised land") and long before his grandchildren would commit "abominations" in the form of freelance polygamy and whoredoms (see Jacob 2:22–35). The monogamy standard subsequently governed the marital practices of Lehi's posterity for a thousand years.

Similarly in the New Testament, Paul taught that bishops were to be "the husband of one wife" (1 Tim. 3:2; Tit. 1:6). After Christ's ascension, Peter held the sealing keys, so eternal marriages could apparently be solemnized, and there were attempts to live some of the higher principles such as the law of consecration (Acts 4:32). Nevertheless, there is no mention of plural marriage, which might have been noted in secular histories at least, if it were practiced among the early Christians.

A review of Church history shows that during the early 1830s, a similar situation occurred. Joseph Smith learned at that time that polygamy was acceptable to God, but that it was not then permitted. In 1832, Joseph told individuals, then in the Church, that he had inquired of the Lord concerning the principle of plurality of wives, and he received for answer that the principle of taking more wives than one is a true principle, but the time had not yet come for it to be practiced.[71]

Latter-day Saints today believe that this same marital directive applies to them. They hold that in 1904, God withdrew the privilege and authorization to practice plural marriage through President Joseph F. Smith, the "one" man then holding the keys of sealing. Hence, from that time forward, plural marriage was *not permitted*.

AT TIMES, PLURAL MARRIAGE IS *PERMITTED*

In contrast to times when God did not allow plural marriage, religious history suggests that seasons existed when it was *permitted*. In such periods, the "one" man holding the keys solemnized plural marriages for worthy men and women who desired to practice polygamy. Saints could also live monogamously without eternal penalty.

Regarding marriage practices in Old Testament times, *Smith's Bible Dictionary* records: "Monogamy [was] the original law of marriage. . . . In the patriarchal age, polygamy prevailed." It appears that "the Mosaic law . . . [was] directed to the discouragement of polygamy." And, "In the post-Babylonian period monogamy appears to have become more prevalent than at any previous time: indeed we have no instance of polygamy during this period on record in the Bible, all the marriages noticed being with single wives. The practice of po-

---

71. As recalled by Orson Pratt, in *Journal of Discourses,* 13:193, October 7, 1869.

lygamy, nevertheless, still existed."[72] Historian Jessie Embry observed: "Polygamy was historically an option, but not a requirement, in Old Testament society."[73]

This situation seems to have recurred in the period between 1890 and 1904. The Latter-day Saints were taught that polygamy was no longer required in order to receive all of the Father's blessings. While 60 percent of the general authorities had children by plural wives during that period, the other 40 percent did not.

As already noted, Church members believe that the 1890 Manifesto was not a directive to refrain from plural marriages. Instead it is seen as a proclamation telling the Latter-day Saints that Heavenly Father had accepted their sacrifice and that plural marriage was no longer *commanded*. However, the actions of Church leaders show that it was still *permitted*. Several hundred authorized plural marriage were secretly allowed between 1890 and 1904. When discovered by non-member politicians and the media, significant problems occurred for the Church and its leaders.

AT TIMES, PLURAL MARRIAGE IS *COMMANDED*

Religious history shows that plural marriage has rarely been *commanded* by God. While the Old Testament states that Abraham took Hagar to wife at Sarah's bidding (Gen. 16:1–3), the Doctrine and Covenants tells us that God required it (D&C 132:34–35). This appears to be the only recorded instance in the scriptures of a man being *commanded* by God to enter into plural marriage.

In Nauvoo, Joseph Smith taught certain Church leaders and members that they were commanded to enter into polygamy. Brigham Young was one of those so instructed and recalled his response: "When I saw a funeral, I felt to envy the corpse its situation, and to regret that I was not in the coffin, knowing

72. J. D. Douglas, et al., *New Bible Dictionary*, 2d ed. (Leicester, Eng.: Inter-Varsity Press, 1962), 742, s.v. "marriage."
73. Jessie L. Embry, *Mormon Polygamous Families: Life in the Principle* (Salt Lake City: University of Utah Press, 1987), 4.

the toil and labor that my body would have to undergo."[74]

For Latter-day Saints, a third example where plural marriage was *commanded* is found between 1852 and 1890. President Young announced the doctrine of polygamy to the world in 1852. For the next thirty-eight years, various priesthood leaders would on occasion teach the Saints that plural marriage was commanded by God. It was a special commandment to Church members of that era with blessings attached.

We do not know why God gave the Latter-day Saints this singular commandment. According to the scriptural record, this thirty-eight year period is the only time any of God's followers have been so commanded in the 6,000-year history of the earth. Accordingly, it seems unlikely that authorized plural marriage itself brings some magical blessing or advantage in time or eternity. Rather, Heavenly Father appears to have desired the Saints of that era to experience the challenges and benefits it then brought to them. The issue was primarily obedience, not polygamy.

PLURAL MARRIAGE	TIME PERIOD
Commanded	• Latter-day Saints 1852–1890 • Abraham • Selected Church Members in Nauvoo
Permitted	• Latter-day Saints 1890–1904 • Old Testament
Not Permitted	• Latter-day Saints after 1904 • Book of Mormon: Lehi • Joseph Smith: early 1830s • New Testament (?)

---

74. Brigham Young, in *Journal of Discourses*, 3:266, July 14, 1855.

Polygamy Continues Outside of the Church and Independent of the "One" Man

Most historians agree that the 1904 "official statement" represents a watershed with respect to plural marriages authorized by the President of the Church, then Joseph F. Smith. Nevertheless, it did not stop new plural marriages from being performed by both Church members and dissenters. To bypass President Joseph F. Smith's refusals to authorize new plural marriages, after 1904, individuals adopted other strategies to ostensibly access valid sealing authority (but they never actually did). During the years immediately after 1904, most participants recognized that without sealing authority from the "one" man mentioned in D&C 132:7, who was the President of the Church, their plural marriages were "not valid, neither of force" in the next life (D&C 132:18).

UNAUTHORIZED APOSTLES, PATRIARCHS, AND TEMPLE SEALERS

Alleged sources of priesthood authorizations included apostles John W. Taylor and Matthias Cowley who, on their own account, permitted several new plural marriages after 1904. As a consequence, they were dropped from the Quorum of the Twelve Apostles in 1906 and experienced further discipline in 1911. In addition, several unauthorized temple sealers feigned authority for new plural sealings.

One interesting source of sealing authority adopted after 1904 was found in the calling of stake patriarchs. The Doctrine and Covenants specifies that the Church patriarch "shall hold the keys of the patriarchal blessings upon the heads of all my people, That whoever he blesses shall be blessed, and whoever he curses shall be cursed; that *whatsoever he shall bind on earth shall be bound in heaven*; and whatsoever he shall loose on earth shall be loosed in heaven . . . [the Church Patriarch holds] *the sealing blessings of my church*, even the Holy Spirit of promise, whereby ye are sealed up unto the day of redemption" (D&C 124: 92–93, 124; italics added). If these three verses were all the instructions available to Latter-day Saints on the subject of sealing authority or the duties of patriarchs, they might possibly assume that a patriarch did indeed have the ability to seal a marriage. However, Church leaders have explained that patriarchs hold "sealing authority" to seal patriarchal blessings upon the heads of Church members.

The problem with patriarchs assuming sealing authority caused President Heber J. Grant to announce in 1921: "We have excommunicated several patriarchs because they arrogated unto themselves, the right, or pretended right, to perform these ceremonies, and after our having excommunicated several patriarchs, another one, so I am informed, has committed the same offense. I announce to all Israel that no living man has the right to perform plural marriages. I announce that no patriarch has the right to perform any marriages at all in the Church."[75]

Importantly, historical records from the 1904 to 1920s period demonstrate conclusively that the scattered plural marriages occurring after the second manifesto were freelanced by the individuals involved. No evidence has been located to support the existence of a formal organization dedicated to the perpetuation of plural marriage during that time. Most signifi-

75. Heber J. Grant, *Conference Report*, April 1921, 220; James R. Clark, ed., *Messages of the First Presidency*, 6 vols. (Salt Lake city: Bookcraft, 1965-71), 5:196.

cantly, no individuals asserted themselves as leaders, presiding over the sealing activities or claiming special authority in or out of the Church.

President Joseph F. Smith died on November 19, 1918. Just prior to his passing, he encouraged his successor, Heber J. Grant, saying: "Always remember this is the Lord's work, and not man's. The Lord is greater than any man. He knows who He wants to lead His Church, and never makes any mistakes."[76] Heber J. Grant would be left with the responsibility of confronting the "fundamentalist" groups that would form during the next two decades.

Polygamous dissenters from the LDS Church underwent a huge transformation in the 1920s. They then began congregating to share their feelings and testimonies, united by the idea that plural marriage needed to be continued. No identifiable leaders would emerge for another decade, but several individuals became prominent within the informal gatherings, either because of their testimonies, convictions, publications, or financial successes, or because of their claims to priesthood authority. Foremost among them was Lorin C. Woolley.

LORIN C. WOOLLEY, A KIND, GENTLE STORYTELLER

Lorin was born in Salt Lake City, Utah, on October 23, 1856, to John Wickersham Woolley and Julia Searles Ensign. Baptized by his father at age thirteen, Church records show that he was ordained an elder on March 10, 1873, by John Lyon.[77] On January 5, 1883, Lorin married Sarah Ann Roberts in the Endowment House on Temple Square and together they had nine children.

Lorin C. Woolley was a kind, gentle storyteller. Beginning in 1921, he related many remarkable tales, most of which

---

76. Quoted in D. Michael Quinn, *The Mormon Hierarchy: Extensions of Power* (Salt Lake City: Signature Books, 1997), 816.
77. Church Membership records of the South Davis Stake.

Lorin C. Woolley

placed him squarely in the limelight. For example, he taught that he was a "thirty-third degree Mason of the Scottish Rites Lodge, Washington, D.C. [and] only one of eight thirty-third degree Masons in all of New York, Washington, D.C., Chicago and St. Louis."[78]

Lorin appears to have had a fancy for governmental leaders. He asserted that he personally converted Teddy Roosevelt to the gospel[79] and that the U.S. President was also a polygamist saying: "Theodore Roosevelt joined Church, received endowments shortly after ascending to Presidency after death of McKinley."[80] Woolley also claimed: "Hoover apparently leans to Catholicism, while Theodore Roosevelt... entered the Patriarchal Order of Marriage (i.e. polygamy)."[81] "He received his endowments under the hands of [John W.] Woolley and Joseph F. Smith in the Black Hills of Wyoming."[82]

Lorin also taught that President Coolidge: "held the Priesthood."[83] Regarding a later president, Franklin D.

78. Joseph White Musser, "Book of Remembrance of Joseph W. Musser," July 30, 1931, 7. Photocopy in author's possession. Abbreviations for cities expanded from initials.

79. Charles W. Kingston, interviewed by Rhea Allred Kunz Baird, October 1971, in Mark J. and Rhea A. Baird , *Reminiscences of John W. and Lorin C. Woolley,* 1st ed., 5 vols. (Payson, Utah: Latter Day Publications, 2007), 3:9; also found in 3:109 of the second edition.

80. Musser, "Book of Remembrance of Joseph W. Musser," November 8, 1932, 45. Abbreviations expanded.

81. Joseph W. Musser, *Items from a Book of Remembrance of Joseph W. Musser* (N.p.: published privately, n.d.), 15.

82. Moroni Jessop, *Testimony of Moroni Jessop* (N.p.: published privately, n.d.), 12; photocopy in author's possession.

83. Musser, "Book of Remembrance of Joseph W. Musser," 53, January 5, 1933; *Items from a Book of Remembrance of Joseph W. Musser,* 22; Baird and Baird, *Reminiscences of John W. and Lorin C. Woolley,* 2d ed., 3:109.

Roosevelt, Woolley explained: "He believes in religious liberty and those who live the Patriarchal Order of Marriage as a religious rite he claims cannot be interfered with under the constitution. He has been consulted and promised to do the right thing if elected."[84] One listener recalled:

> Lorin C. Woolley was asked in October of 1932, "Whom would you advise us to vote for?" He replied that he should not tell people how to vote, that *he had promised F.D. Roosevelt personally that he would give him his vote*, but," said Bro. Woolley, "I had my reasons for promising that, but I'm not advising you to vote for him. I'll tell you this much, if he is elected he will bring things to a head quicker." We plainly understood this statement presaged evil, and yet we knew it had to come to fulfill prophecy. (Italics added.)[85]

Another witness remembered: "Lorin told me never to say anything against [Mahatma Gandhi]. He turned to me and said...'I tell you, Mahatma Gandhi is a prophet of God. Don't you ever say anything against him. I am personally acquainted with him. The world does not know he is a prophet of God.'"[86]

Woolley taught in 1922 that he "had been a government official and as such had learned many things about the brethren who are now so pronounced against the principle of plural marriage."[87] Specifically, Lorin taught that he had learned of post-manifesto plural marriages of Church leaders through his activities as an agent of the Secret Service of the United States

84. Musser, "Book of Remembrance of Joseph W. Musser," 37, September 2, 1932; *Items from a Book of Remembrance of Joseph W. Musser,* 23.

85. Baird and Baird, *Reminiscences of John W. and Lorin C. Woolley,* 1st ed., 5:27 note 1.

86. Jessop, *Testimony of Moroni Jessop,* 22.

87. Joseph Musser, Journal, April 9, 1922; photocopy in author's possession.

of America, having been commissioned in 1890 to spy upon them and monitor their activities.

One follower recalled: "Porter Rockwell, who was also working on the underground for the Kingdom of God, died June 9, 1878. Lorin C. Woolley then took his place."[88] And: "Lorin was selected when a young man to join the Secret Service of the United States, and became before his death, one of the greatest mortal detectives in modern times. He told me while working for him and living with him of many dangerous exploits he had."[89] Another supporter remembered that "Lorin Woolley explained that he was brought into the Secret Service by President Theodore Roosevelt and worked up to the position of Major."[90]

A review of Lorin's life fails to reveal any occasion when he might have participated in Masonry as he reported, and the Secret Service denied that he was ever an agent or employee. His claims that U.S. Presidents were Church members or polygamists are contradicted by plain historical facts. Lorin Woolley's reported interactions with U.S. Presidents greatly contrast Joseph Smith's own encounter with President Martin Van Buren in November 1839. Van Buren treated Joseph "very insolently" telling him, "your cause is just, but I can do nothing for you."[91]

Lorin C. Woolley also professed many interactions with resurrected beings. He told of a vision he had received when on his mission to the Indian Territory at the age of about thirty. He had then become seriously ill and was visited by Jesus Christ,

88. Jessop, *Testimony of Moroni Jessop*, 9.
89. Ibid., 6.
90. Fred Cleveland, interview, in Lynn L. Bishop, *The 1886 Visitations of Jesus Christ and Joseph Smith to John Taylor: the Centerville Meetings* (Salt Lake City: Latter Day Publications, 1998), 172.
91. Joseph Smith Jr. *History of The Church of Jesus Christ of Latter-day Saints,* ed. B. H. Roberts, 2d ed., rev., 7 vols. (Salt Lake City: Deseret Book, 1971), 4:80.

Joseph Smith, and John Taylor. Ultimately, John Taylor blessed Lorin, and he was healed. Lorin claimed to have met the Savior many times, as well as Joseph Smith, Brigham Young, John Taylor, and Heber C. Kimball, all as resurrected beings.

One listener recalled Lorin's teachings regarding Moroni, son of Mormon: "He told me he had seen him. He said he is a little larger man than either Joseph Smith or the Savior. He said, he had almost a straight nose and blue eyes. He was a little broader shouldered. All three men, Joseph, the Savior and Moroni—all were blue eyed men. Lorin said, 'The Savior's hair was a deep auburn. Joseph's hair was a dark auburn.'"[92] On another occasion "Lorin C. Woolley said to some friends that the remark about Jesus never laughing was not true, 'For, I have seen him laugh.'"[93]

Most of the men and women who listened to Lorin Woolley teach in the 1920s and 1930s remember him sharing stories about his visits to the Yucatan peninsula in Mexico. Reportedly, one such visit occurred the night of April 7, 1932. Joseph Musser, a follower of Woolley, recorded the following account the morning after the alleged visit occurred:

> During last night, [Lorin Woolley] at home of J. Leslie Broadbent, claims to have been visited and conversed one-half or three-quarters of an hour with one of the three Nephite Apostles and was by him conducted to a temple in Yucatan, South America, [sic], that was built shortly after the days of the Savior in mortality. Its about the size and architectural design as the Salt Lake Temple. No ordinance work is being done in it, but apparently three Lamanite chiefs have charge of it. It is miraculously kept clean. Its location is not known by the nations generally. One of the chiefs spoke of having seven wives and one five. . . . While there [Lorin] was introduced to a congregation of about 300 people—who

92. Jessop, *Testimony of Moroni Jessop*, 41.
93. Baird, *Reminiscences of John W. and Lorin C. Woolley.*, 5:34.

> were awaiting instructions on the gospel. . . . [Lorin]
> was previously taken there and introduced to the leaders
> by the Prophet Joseph Smith under the direction of our
> Lord. These people at Yucatan are white, having Neph-
> ite blood predominating in them. They are intelligent
> and fine people.[94]

As with Lorin's other claims, no substantiating evidence has been located. Extensive geographic mapping and exploration of the Yucatan peninsula has been undertaken. Nevertheless, no temple or Indian people remotely matching Lorin's narrative have been found. The Church of Jesus Christ of Latter-day Saint dedicated the Mérida Mexico Temple on July 8, 2000.

Lorin also made a number of prophesies and many fantastic declarations on a variety of subjects. As can be imagined, His teachings greatly impressed his audiences in the 1920s. Unfortunately for believers today, none of Lorin's prophecies came true and his other assertions remain unconfirmed and generally contradicted by all available research.

Over the past few decades, Mormon fundamentalist leaders have been reticent to publish Lorin's instructions as recorded by Joseph Musser and others. Censored versions have been made available, but full transcripts of known documents have been shared with very few. For a detailed review of many of Lorin's teachings, see *Modern Polygamy and Mormon Fundamentalism: The Generations After the Manifesto* (Salt Lake City: Greg Kofford Books, 2006), 145–75.

Of all of Lorin Woolley's recollections and claims, none was more significant than the one that asserted priesthood authority to perform eternal polygamous sealings.

---

94. Musser, "Book of Remembrance of Joseph W. Musser," April 8, 1932, 21–22,

An Independent "Priesthood Organization" Disclosed

In the 1930s, Lorin C. Woolley disclosed a new and revolutionary teaching regarding priesthood authority and the organizations that preside within it.

A "PRIESTHOOD" ORGANIZATION, THE COUNCIL OF FRIENDS, AND HIGH PRIEST APOSTLES

Without a doubt the most important story told by Lorin C. Woolley involved an ordination that reportedly occurred on September 27, 1886. Lorin taught that he was then ordained to a previously unheard of priesthood office called "High Priest Apostle" and thereby became a member of a previously unheard of priesthood council called "The Council of Seven Friends." According to Lorin Woolley, this council existed outside of the Church as part of a "priesthood" organization that existed independent of all other religious entities. Woolley taught that the council was more powerful than any priesthood quorum within the Church including the First Presidency. It also directed the kingdom of God through a Council of Fifty. According to Lorin, the "priesthood" also contained a Sanhedrin of seventy members, although he never attempted to organize it.

Reportedly, the senior member of the Council of Seven Friends is the "one" man holding the keys of sealing. Lorin taught that the Council of Seven Friends had secretly existed since 1829 and had actually been running the Church and kingdom of God throughout the ensuing decades. Ostensibly, Joseph Smith, Brigham Young, and John Taylor presided, not because they were the senior apostle and President of the Church in their times, but because they secretly held this higher office in the covert Council of Seven Friends.

Lorin's declaration that the Council of Seven Friends had always existed outside of the Church and presided over it is problematic. No evidence has been located to supports his claim, and the entity was unheard of prior to 1930 when Lorin first mentioned it. If it ever existed or met in council, no minutes of their meetings have been discovered. Journal entries written by alleged Council of Seven members never referred to it or its decisions or intentions.

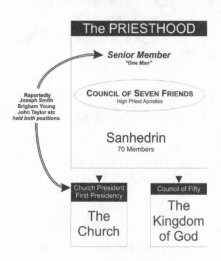

The PRIESTHOOD
(Woolley, Barlow, Musser 1934)

tentions. Many historians, including myself and D. Michael Quinn, have diligently searched for any sign of a Council of Seven Friends existing prior to 1930. No signs have been found.[95]

Joseph Smith taught that God's Church exists wherever a man or woman repents and is baptized. Doctrine & Covenants 10:67–68 specifies: "Behold, this is my doctrine—whosoever repenteth and cometh unto me, the same is my church. Whosoever declareth more or less than this, the same is not of me, but is against me; therefore he is not of my church." Accordingly, the idea that a man could hold the priesthood and preside over the Church without being a member of the Church

95. I discussed this personally with D. Michael Quinn on May 10, 2006.

is unique and unsupported. Heber C. Kimball taught in 1852: "When a man loses his membership in this Church, he also loses his Priesthood."[96]

FIVE MEN ORDAINED
WITH SUPERIOR PRIESTHOOD POWER?

Besides Lorin's alleged 1886 ordination, he also recalled that four other men were similarly ordained at that time. However, Lorin waited until the other four were dead before making the claim. This contrasts D&C 6:28: "in the mouth of two or three witnesses shall every word be established." When important priesthood ordinations oc-

John W. Woolley

curred, at least two witnesses were present. For the bestowal of the Aaronic Priesthood (D&C 13:1), the Melchizedek Priesthood (D&C 27:12), and important keys of the priesthood (D&C 110:11–13), both Joseph Smith and Oliver Cowdery were there bearing witness. No one else has ever corroborated Lorin's story of these important ordinations.

Reportedly, "the Prophet Joseph Smith stood by directing the proceedings" as the ordinations were performed. One of the other four men was Lorin's father, John W. Woolley. Reportedly John was the first man to served as God's prophet and not be the President of The Church of Jesus Christ of Latterday Saints. Lorin stated that John had been the senior member of the Council of Seven Friends for many years before his 1928 death, though precisely when the sealing keys reportedly left the Church to reside in his keeping is a point of confusion.

Regardless, when John W. Woolley was excommunicated in 1914, he made no claims to an 1886 ordination or asserted

96. Heber C. Kimball, in *Journal of Discourses* 26 vols. (Liverpool: F. D. Richards, 1855–86), 3:269, March 23, 1856.

that he was a member of a secret Priesthood Council and was actually in charge of all priesthood in or out of the Church. One follower recalled: "John W. Woolley would not preside in any meeting outside of his own home."[97] John attempted to keep his Church membership and was distraught over his excommunication. His actions show that he respected President Joseph F. Smith as the presiding priesthood leader on earth, even though Joseph F. Smith started the process through which John was cut off. After President Smith's death, John appealed to Heber J. Grant's authority to be reinstated. Nothing in John Woolley's behavior suggested that he held the lofty position Lorin would later claim for him. John himself was a monogamist most of his life, having two wives for a brief six years between 1886 and 1892.

Two of the other men listed as being ordained with Lorin were Samuel Bateman and Charles Wilken.[98] Both were serving as bodyguards to the Church leaders. Why they would have been instantly elevated to a super-powerful authoritative council in

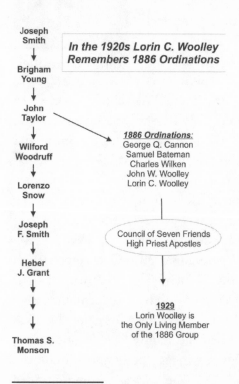

In the 1920s Lorin C. Woolley Remembers 1886 Ordinations

Joseph Smith
↓
Brigham Young
↓
John Taylor
↓
Wilford Woodruff
↓
Lorenzo Snow
↓
Joseph F. Smith
↓
Heber J. Grant
↓
↓
Thomas S. Monson

1886 Ordinations:
George Q. Cannon
Samuel Bateman
Charles Wilken
John W. Woolley
Lorin C. Woolley

Council of Seven Friends
High Priest Apostles

1929
Lorin Woolley is the Only Living Member of the 1886 Group

---

97. Price Johnson, in Mark J. and Rhea A. Baird , *Reminiscences of John W. and Lorin C. Woolley,* 2nd ed., 5 vols. (Payson, Utah: Latter Day Publications, 2007), 2:65.

98. Also spelled Wilcken or Wilkins.

1886 to preside over all other priesthood leaders was never explained. Bateman kept a journal that contains no mention of any special ordination then or at any time during his life. His numerous hand-written entries include no references to activities consistent with a high priesthood calling or membership in a secret priesthood council. The historical record fails to identify even one marriage (monogamist or polygamist) performed by either Bateman or Wilken and shows they both obeyed the 1890 Manifesto.

The fifth individual listed by Lorin was First Counselor in the First Presidency George Q. Cannon. As an apostle, he already possessed all priesthood authority that could be bestowed and would have nothing to benefit by an additional ordination.

Woolley also reported that prior to the alleged ordinations, an eight-hour meeting was held with thirteen people in attendance. During that meeting, John Taylor reportedly floated above the floor and made everyone covenant to continue polygamy no matter what happened. Of the thirteen people named, three kept journals. Their entries for that date (and surrounding dates) are consistent with each other and contain no mention of any meeting. Examining the lives of the other twelve individuals provides little or no evidence that they experienced a spiritual theophany or received such a strict commission that day.

INVESTIGATING THE ORIGIN OF LORIN'S PRIESTHOOD ORGANIZATION

As reviewed above, nothing has been found in the historical record to support Lorin C. Woolley's reported ordination as a High Priest Apostle or his teachings of an external priesthood organization with a Council of Seven Friends. If they did not exist until the twentieth century, what other explanation might account for their origin and their true relationship to the Church?

Many years ago, an episode of the TV western "Bonanza" involved an old settler named Charlie Parsons, who discovered that his cattle were disappearing into thin air. He made sure that all of his cows were branded with his own CP brand, so they might be easily identified, but the disappearances continued. Parsons would count his cattle in the evening, but by morning, a few would be missing. He recruited the help of everyone in the area including the Cartwrights, but no one could find any stray cattle with the CP brand.

Just a month before the problem started, a new neighbor Gilbert R. Ellison had moved in, setting up his ranch right next to Parsons. As it turned out, Gilbert R. Ellison was a crook. He had created his own GRE brand that could be easily superimposed on top of Parson's CP brand. At night, Ellison would grab a few of Parson's animals and then rebrand them with his own GRE symbol. In the morning, all the cattle in Ellison's corrals were properly branded "GRE," and Parson was left scratching his head trying to figure out what happened. Of course, with the help of the Cartwrights, the mystery was solved and justice was served—all by the final commercial.

It seems possible that Lorin C. Woolley may have treated the Church like Gilbert R. Ellison treated Charlie Parson's cattle. To legitimize his position outside and superior to the Church, he superimposed his external priesthood offices and councils over the Church, offices and councils that were not part of the original organization restored through Joseph Smith:

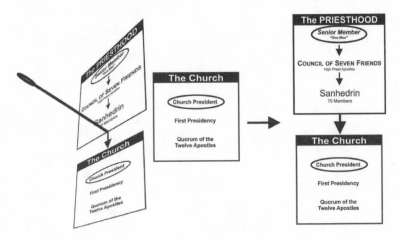

Despite important identifiable problems with Lorin C. Woolley and his teachings, his claims to sealing priesthood authority serve as the source for most Mormon fundamentalist groups today, including the FLDS (Warren Jeffs) and the Allred Group. However, most Mormon fundamentalists have discarded the teachings of High Priest Apostles and the Council of Seven Friends as Woolley originally described them, even though they represent the root source of the authority they utilize in their marriage sealings.

Lorin Wooley Calls Men to Fill His Council of Seven Friends

As noted above, Lorin waited until all of the other four men he claimed were Council of Seven Friends members had died before teaching about the council or naming them as participants. In fact, research fails to identify any reference to the Council of Seven Friends by Lorin Woolley or anyone else prior to 1932. In any case, for reasons Lorin never explained, God allowed this super-powerful priesthood council to dwindle to only one member before requiring additional new High Priest Apostles be called.

Lousis Kelsch, Joseph Musser, J. Leslie Broadbent, Lorin C. Woolley, and friend

Lorin called six men to fill the vacancies between 1929 and 1933.

J. Leslie Broadbent	March 6, 1929 (first)
John Y. Barlow	March 6, 1929 (second)
Joseph W. Musser	May 14, 1929
Charles F. Zitting	July 22, 1932 (first)
Legrand Woolley	July 22,1932 (second)
Louis Kelsch	January 26, 1933

Originally, Broadbent, Barlow, and Musser received "blessings" that were only later described as "ordinations to the Council of Seven Friends."[99] It appears that prior to 1932, Woolley withheld many details regarding this all-powerful priesthood quorum.

Once the Council of Seven Friends doctrine had been established, council members went forth to teach fellow polygamists regarding it. No one had ever heard of the idea prior to the 1930s, so even the eager pluralists were in the dark. During the next decade, Joseph Musser noted several times in his journal that he spent time teaching his fellow fundamentalists about the priesthood "set-up" or "situation."[100] By the mid-1930s, a majority of polygamists had united behind the priesthood claims of those men, although many followers rejected the priesthood hierarchy as described. By 1940, the Council of Seven Friends was usually referred to as simply the "Priesthood Council."

J. Leslie Broadbent

Lorin died in 1934, and J. Leslie Broadbent presided for a short six months before succumbing to pneumonia. Then John Y. Barlow eagerly took hold of the reins. Within months he and Joseph Musser visited Short Creek, Arizona, an area on the Utah-Arizona boarder fifty miles east of St. George. It would soon become an outpost and then the center of polygamist activities for a large number of plural marriage proponents.

99. See Joseph Musser, Journals, May 14, 1929, Church Archives. Copy of holograph in possession of the author.
100. Ibid., the "priesthood set-up" is mentioned in December 1, 1936; October 3, 1937; December 8, 1938; April 26, November 5, 1939, and the "priesthood situation" in July 23, 1939.

1936: "WHERE ARE THE KEYS OF SEALING?"

Shortly after visiting Short Creek, John Y. Barlow moved there with his families. As the senior High Priest Apostle, he presided over all activities, but problems soon arose due to his autocratic behavior. In response to numerous complaints, Joseph Musser and Louis Kelsch visited from Salt Lake City. Musser wrote on November 8, 1936:

> Thursday Louis Kelsch and I had a personal talk with Bro. John Y. Barlow. We pointed out our fears that under the present set-up the group could not prosper; that there seemed a disposition toward a one man rule; that the present arrangement was not in accordance with the spirit of the action of the Priesthood recently taken, whereby it was advised that Bro. Barlow resign from the Management of the affairs of the group and confine his labors more particularly to the spiritual field; that our work was especially along the line of keeping faith in patriarchal marriage alive, and not in the directing of colonizing.
>
> *Bro. Barlow was asked if he claimed to hold the keys of Priesthood, which he answered in the negative,* saying, however, that he had dreamed of a personage coming to him and handing him a bunch of keys, and leaving without explanation. He did not know that that had any special significance (italics added).[101]

Barlow's admission regarding his lack of priesthood keys created doubt and confusion among his followers. A few days passed, and Musser attempted to assuage these concerns:

> The majority expressed the belief that Brother John Y. Barlow held the keys to Priesthood and was the mouth-piece of God on earth, and with some this was the only reason for accepting Bro. Barlow's Management of affairs. Elders Covington and I. W. Barlow expressed emphatic dissent, stating they did not believe

---

101. Ibid., November 8, 1936.

Brother Barlow held the keys to Priesthood, but that he did have authority to seal and was the senior member in the Priesthood group, and as such presided at the meetings of the group, etc.

J. W. Musser explained his views on Priesthood matters: That the special mission and labors of the Priesthood group were to keep plural marriage alive; that we were not called upon to colonize only as the Lord might dictate such a move . . . That the time had not come for the establishing of the united order.

Stated *the Lord had not revealed to him* [Joseph Musser] *who held the Keys to Priesthood*, but that Bro. Barlow, by reason of his seniority in ordination presided over the group; that questions pertaining to the mission of the group, when acted upon by unanimous vote, were properly settled and such action became the word of the Lord upon the points thus involved (italics added).[102]

John Y. Barlow

During this episode, John Y. Barlow and Joseph Musser explained to their listeners that neither of them held the keys of the priesthood. These plain admissions have not deterred thousands of modern Mormon fundamentalist polygamists from disagreeing, affirming that in fact Barlow did hold the sealing keys in 1936 and beyond. Apparently he was just unaware. This paradox persists and is difficult to explain.

GOVERNMENTAL RAID, IMPRISONMENT, AND A MANIFESTO

As leader of the polygamist organization, Barlow proceeded to call new members to the Priesthood Council, including Leroy Johnson and Marion Hammon, who were ordained in 1941. Four years later, Rulon Jeffs, Guy Musser, and Richard

102. Ibid., November 13, 1936.

Jessop were called. Then, in 1946, Carl Holm was set apart and three years following, Alma Timpson. Surprisingly, this council, which was described by Woolley as having seven men (he often referred to it as simply "the Seven"), then had twelve members.

In 1942, Barlow instigated the organization of the United Effort Plan or UEP. It started as an attempt to live the united order, but as it evolved, it also became a tool for polygamist leaders to exercise control over the property and houses of their followers. While the services of a "bishop's storehouse" (run by Fred Jessop) assisted many Short Creek pluralists with daily commodities and other needs, the UEP bore little resemblance

Convicted polygamists, 1945. Front left: Oswald Brainich, Joseph W. Musser, Louis A. Kelsch, Dr. Rulon C. Allred, Albert E. Barlow, Ianthus W. Barlow, John Y. Barlow, and Edmund F. Barlow. Back left: David B. Darger, Charles F. Zitting, Joseph Lyman Jessop, Heber K. Cleveland, Arnold Boss, Alma A. Timpson, and Morris Q. Kunz.

to the law of consecration as described in the Doctrine and Covenants (see 42:30–39).

Government officials were not ignorant of the growing polygamy presence on the Utah-Arizona border. By January 1944, Musser learned the "The F.B.I [was] making a desperate attempt to get something on Brother Barlow and myself to prosecute us in the courts." While believing the Church was behind the move, he seemed undaunted: "Let them investigate and be dammed and go to hell if they choose to, the work of the Lord will not stop."[103] As the tensions mounted, he reflected: "Some of us may have to go to prison, but what of that. We should be willing to bear such a testimony to the nation if that course is the will of the Lord."[104]

On March 7, 1944, at 6:00 a.m., heavily armed lawmen swooped down on the inhabitants of Short Creek, as well as homes of fundamentalists in Salt Lake City and other locations in Arizona, Utah, and Idaho. Musser recalled that the policemen continued their search of his home "until about 11:00 a.m. when the officers took me to the county jail. Arriving there, I found a large congregation of my brethren, who had also been arrested. Of the Priesthood Council, were John Y. Barlow, myself, Charles F. Zitting, LeGrand Woolley, Louis A. Kelsch, also Guy H. Musser and Rulon T. Jeffs, who afterwards became members of the Council."[105] In all, thirty-four men and women were arrested for illegal cohabitation, and fifteen would be convicted.

Notwithstanding an initial excitement and even optimism, prison life quickly took its toll on the seventy-three-year-old Joseph Musser and seventy-one-year-old John Y. Barlow. After six weeks in the pen, Musser complained: "If I have to stay

103. Ibid., January 29, 1944.
104. Ibid., February 29, 1944.
105. Joseph White Musser, *Journal of Joseph White Musser 1872–1954* (N.p.: Pioneer Press, ca. 1948), 13.

here much longer, I believe it will kill me."[106] After about two months of confinement, the group's historian recorded:

> This morning Joseph [Musser] came to my cell door shortly after I arose. He looked very pale. I said kindly, "Joseph, how are you?" He replied, "Well, not so good. I found myself on the floor this morning, when I came to. I guess I must have fainted in the night. It is so hot." He sat on my bed then. I tried to console him. His lips quivered with motion. The left side of his face had three bar marks where the blood had come on through a bruise. The skin was not broken. He said, "but I guess it is all right, anyhow we have got to endure it."
>
> Sometime later . . . Brother [Dell] Timpson said to Joseph, "You are not getting the right kind of food." We asked, "Can we bring you anything?" He replied, "Oh how I would like a good T-bone steak well done and a good glass of beer." He said to me, "I would like to be home in a soft bed, the doors to the house closed and no one allowed to come in and just rest and rest." His lips quivered as he tried to speak.[107]

Three days passed and council leaders Barlow and Musser summoned twelve of the fifteen offenders to a special meeting. There a manifesto was presented to the men:

> *To whom it may concern*:
>
> The undersigned officers and members of the so-called Fundamentalist religious group desiring to bring about peace and harmony within the Church, and recognizing the futility of disobeying the laws of the land even in the practice of a religious belief, do hereby declare as follows:
>
> That we individually and severally pledge ourselves to refrain hereafter from advocating, teaching or coun-

---

106. Arnold Boss, *Prison Diary of Arnold Boss: From May 15, 1945 to December 15, 1947* (Salt Lake City: published privately , ca. 1980), July 27, 1945.

107. Ibid., August 18, 1945.

tenancing the practice of plural marriage or polygamy, in violation of the laws of the State of Utah and the United States.

The undersigned officers of the religious group above referred to, further pledge ourselves to refrain from engaging in or solemnizing plural marriages from and after this date.[108]

Ultimately, a division occurred within the group with four men defying John Y. Barlow's direct instructions to sign the manifesto, among them was council member Charles Zitting. Eleven of the men were paroled after six months, and the other four were released a couple of years later. Most of the men resumed their polygamist activities upon leaving prison.

---

108. Ibid., August 21, 1945.

Joseph Musser Presides and the Fundamentalists Split

For a couple of decades between 1930 and 1950, the modern polygamists enjoyed relative unity and expansion. John Y. Barlow died on December 29, 1949, leaving Joseph Musser to preside over the eleven-member Priesthood Council and a few thousand followers. Within three years, Musser's leadership decisions would divide the fundamentalists forever.

MUSSER PRESIDES AND THE FUNDAMENTALISTS SPLIT

Shortly before Barlow's death, Musser experienced a stroke and called upon polygamist naturopath Rulon Allred for medical care. After joining the fundamentalists in 1935, Allred had made a favorable impression on Barlow, who ordained him to special work within the group. Musser was also impressed with Allred and despite his stroke-induced handicaps, ordained Allred on September 18, 1950, saying:

> "I have prayed concerning this matter for a long time and thought somewhat of calling my son Guy as my Second Elder, but I was not impressed to do it. I am going to ordain you to that calling." Musser then arose from his bed, placing his feet on the side and told Rulon to kneel down close to him. Placing his hands on Rulon's head he pronounced a blessing: "Brother Rulon C. Allred, by virtue of my Apostleship, I lay my hands upon your head and set you apart to be my First Coun-

selor and to stand at my side as Hyrum stood to Joseph and as Leslie [Broadbent] stood to Lorin [Woolley].[109]

Musser's words on this occasion created confusion. It appeared that Musser was telling his polygamist followers, in-

Joseph W. Musser

cluding members of the Priesthood Council, that at his death, Allred would succeed him as the leader of the fundamentalists. Members of the Priesthood Council were distraught upon learning of the proceedings. They universally felt that Musser could not, without their approval, call additional members of the Priesthood Council. Frustrations escalated since they were neither consulted regarding the calling, nor invited to participate in the original ordination. They were suspicious regarding Musser's sanity and Allred's motives.

Ultimately, the council members rejected Allred as anything more than a private counselor to Joseph Musser who would be released at Musser's death. In response, in January of 1952, Musser released all the members of the Priesthood Council previously called by John Y. Barlow. Importantly, he utilized his position as the "senior member" of the council to call and set apart seven new members: Rulon C. Allred, Elsie Jensen, John Butchereit, Lyman Jessop, Owen Allred, Marvin Allred, and Joseph B. Thompson, as replacements. Lorin C. Woolley's High Priest Apostles Charles Zitting, LeGrand Woolley and Louis Kelsch were left in limbo.

In Musser's eyes these seven men comprised the true Priesthood Council, displacing the old council members who had

---

109. Melba F. Allred, "Items Concerning Priesthood," as quoted in Gilbert Fulton, ed. *Gems,* 3 vols. (Salt Lake City: Gems Publishing, 1967), 2:33–35.

opposed him. Accordingly, members of the old council were expected to follow the new Priesthood Council that Musser had just assembled. In August, Musser affirmed: "Whatever his former council did, was without authority from now on, unless he [Musser] sanctioned it and then it is done by HIS authority, not their own" (emphasis in original).[110]

Understandably, old council members refused to be released even though Joseph Musser supported only the second, newer group. Even his own son, Guy Musser, opposed him saying: "Brother Allred is a devil. He has tried for the last fifteen years to split up the Priesthood. My father is incompetent and is not able to give any man the Apostleship. Rulon has not got it. All that follow R. C. Allred, work under a spurious Priesthood and all his work done is unauthorized. . . . Some of the brethren have tried to put me next to father, but I am seventh in

Back - Louis Kelsch, Charles Zitting. Front - John Y. Barlow, Joseph Musser

the line down. My father cannot bypass his whole Council and put someone else ahead. . . . The Council of the Priesthood is united in its stand against Brother Allred."[111]

Fundamentalists in Salt Lake City split their support about 50-50 between the two Priesthood Councils. However, the Short Creek polygamists were unanimous in sustaining the older council. Musser, accompanied by new council member J. Lyman Jessop, visited Short Creek in July of 1952. Meeting with Leroy Johnson, Richard Jessop, and Carl Holm of the old council, Lyman Jessop recorded: "Brother Joseph [Musser]

110. Joseph Thompson, Diary, August 24, 1952.
111. Melba Allred, quoted in Fulton, *Gems,* 1:41.

asked Roy [Leroy Johnson] to state how he felt toward him, so Roy said that he knows that Joseph holds the keys to the Priesthood and he [Roy] will sustain him in that position in love and loyalty." Then Johnson stated: "I stood by John [Barlow] until the end. I will support you as I did him."[112]

Musser requested that a meeting be held, and he be allowed to address the Short Creek fundamentalists. Despite the allegiance previously professed, Leroy Johnson refused, saying, "We are under covenant to do what we are doing and we cannot change from that course and we have no arguments to make." Musser was greatly disappointed and replied, "Well, you just as well go your way and we'll go our way."[113] Privately Johnson confided: "If the Lord wants to use an incapacitated leader to lead some people astray, that is the Lord's business."[114]

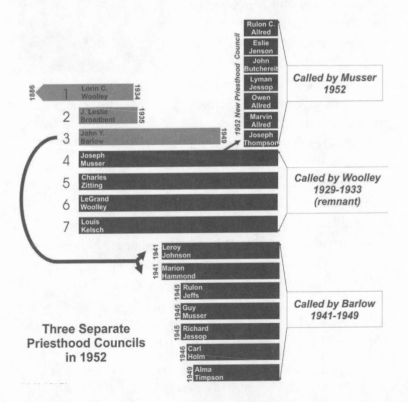

Three Separate Priesthood Councils in 1952

The two Priesthood Councils and the polygamist "groups" that followed them were officially divided. Joseph Musser journeyed north to Salt Lake City, never again to return to Short Creek.

Mid-July 1952 saw a very unique situation in the history of Mormon fundamentalism. Three separate Priesthood Councils could be identified, and all three essentially operated independent of each other.

Joseph Musser passed away on March 29, 1954. Technically, at that point, Charles F. Zitting presided. But Zitting had never asserted himself as a presiding leader, having accumulated some wealth and ten wives, he remained aloof from the United Effort Plan and many of the other projects promoted by Barlow and Musser. Regardless, Zitting himself died just a few months later on July 14. At this point, two of Lorin Woolley's High Priest Apostles were still living, Legrand Woolley and Louis Kelsch, but both refused to assume leadership of the polygamists. This left Leroy Johnson presiding with the Barlow-appointed Priesthood Council in Short Creek, and Rulon Allred firmly in control in the Priesthood Council chosen by Musser.

Short Creek Polygamy Continues

Firmly split from Joseph Musser and Rulon Allred, Leroy S. Johnson and all Short Creek fundamentalists began to expand their polygamist enclave through the United Effort Plan. Unfortunately, they experienced a significant set back in 1953 as Arizona officials raided their little town.

THE 1953 ARIZONA RAID

Elected governor of Arizona in 1950, Howard Pyle heard complaints from cattlemen and other tax-paying citizens in the region of Short Creek, saying that the fundamentalists paid little or no taxes themselves but expected substantial state support in educating their broods of children. In response to these issues and others, Pyle hired the Burns Detective Agency of Los Angeles to investigate the possible polygamous activities alleged to be occurring there. Members of the agency approached the town purporting to be a movie studio looking for people to play the part of "extras" in upcoming movies and were permitted to photograph every citizen and family in the community.

Pyle examined the black and white photographs and expressed his concern. Poverty appeared rampant, and there were questions about the appropriate use of state funds in some of the government-sponsored programs there. The governor learned that the average age for first marriages for fundamentalist women then was sixteen years old, although girls as young as fourteen and fifteen were known to be married. The average age for their first childbirth was seventeen, requiring some teenage girls to obtain release time from school during the day in order to return home to nurse their babies. Pyle decided to prosecute and a secret raid was planned.

"On the 26th of July, 1953, in the dark, but early hours of the morning, storm-troopers under the direction and command of Governor Pyle of Arizona, swooped down upon the peaceful Short Creek community... With guns bristling and leveled at women and children, and with their badges all nice and shiny, and worn in the most conspicuous place, this invading army brought fright and enforced marshal law, to one of the most peaceful and modest communities of Americans in the United States."[115] Sheriff Fred Porter exited the lead car as

1953 Raid, a tent was set up in the center of town.

115. "Oh America: Land of the Free—Home of the Brave—Where Art Thou?" *Truth* 19, no. 4 (September 1953): 97.

Leroy Johnson approached him saying, "We're going to stand right here and shed our blood."[116] Doubtless he meant what he said; thankfully, no blood was spilt.

Over 100 armed men participated, accompanied by "twenty-five car loads" of newspapermen, cameramen, and representatives of the national wire services and magazines who recorded a blow-by-blow account. A large tent was raised in the center of town and barbwire fences were used to segregate the 122 adults and 263 children who were apprehended, virtually every man, woman, and child in the community save six who were not fundamentalists. Of the women between the ages of fourteen and seventeen who were taken into custody, at least twelve were either pregnant or already the mother of several children.

In all, 36 men were arrested and over 190 women and children were taken into custody. Besides the obvious problems arising from the arrest of peaceful citizens, the confinement of females and minors brought a national backlash. Ultimately, Governor Pyle was not re-elected, and all of the individuals detained were restored to Short Creek—despite their continued practice of polygamy.

Leroy Johnson

On the Utah side of the border, Governor J. Bracken Lee was invited to participate in the raid. He declined saying, "You do whatever you have to do but we're not going to become involved."[117] Utah politicians sought to avoid the de-

---

116. Martha Sonntag Bradley, "The Women of Fundamentalism: Short Creek, 1953," *Dialogue: A Journal of Mormon Thought* 23 (Summer 1990): 30.

117. Martha Sonntag Bradley, *Kidnapped from That Land: The Government Raids on the Short Creek Polygamists* (Salt Lake City: University of Utah Press, 1993), 119.

bacle of group arrests, so the Utah Juvenile Court chose to prosecute a "test case" involving Leonard and Vera Black. Leonard was a polygamous husband of three wives, and twenty-six children, Vera the mother of eight of those children. An evaluation of the Black home found that the children's minimal physical necessities were being provided, with no evidence to support an accusation of physical neglect. Though poverty was the norm, it was not a crime.

Throughout the investigation, the crucial issue involved was the polygamous relationship of Leonard and Vera. Since polygamy was illegal, the question boiled down to would the Blacks' willingness to teach their children to break the law suspend their rights as parents to those children? After hearing the evidence, the judge believed that "the only way that the children of these polygamous families can be prevented from going into polygamy is by permanently separating them from their parents at a fairly young age, so that they will not be exposed to the fanatic religious teachings." Consequently, he ruled that the Black home was an "immoral environment for rearing of the children."[118]

A decree was issued on May 11, 1954, declaring that because the Black children were being taught to break the law, they were "neglected" as defined by Utah state law. Consequently, they should be taken from their parents and placed under the care of the Utah Department of Public Welfare. This extreme ruling eventually prompted Vera to sign a statement saying that she would comply with the law, thus allowing her to regain custody of her children.

Due to the perceived stigma associated with the 1953 raids at Short Creek, the name of the community was changed to Colorado City in 1963. Over the decades, they began to refer to themselves as the Fundamentalist Church of Jesus Christ of

118. Ibid., 171.

Latter-day Saints or FLDS Church. By then, people were prospering little by little with the population expanding to over five hundred inhabitants. They implemented the "work mission," which required young men to serve for two years, not as missionaries preaching the gospel, but as employees earning the highest possible wages and sending all of their payroll checks directly to their priesthood leaders. They were to be supported by their families from home. After their two-year service, they would return to Short Creek and receive a wife and building lot.

THE LAW OF PLACING

One teaching that is unique to the FLDS Church involves the "Law of Placing." Considered a "high and holy law," it requires "young ladies [who are] anxious to marry, to submit themselves to the leadership and their father for direction and *placement* into a marriage of divine choosing." The Law of Placing has its roots in the belief of the premortal existence. One fundamentalist leader taught:

> You young people here today are blessed. Many of you are children of the covenant, were chosen from the other side to come down through your parents to carry on this special priesthood work and calling. Some of you young ladies are quick to run about trying to find a husband or you young men run without being sent to find a wife with little or no thought of preserving your birthright amongst the saints and the covenant you have made in the pre-existence. The Lord would have you at this time seek to bring yourselves to the feet of the priesthood, that the mind and will of the Lord may be made known as to whom you have made covenants with on the other side [in the premortal spirit world].[119]

---

119. Kaziah May Hancock, *Prisons of the Mind* (West Jordan, Utah: Desert Blossom, 1987), 64. Hancock uses the pseudonym of "President Tellason" for the speaker, who is undoubtedly Leroy Johnson.

While older men benefited from the Law of Placing, young men sometimes find themselves in a *no man's land* in the community. Their hopes of marrying a suitable wife upon arriving at normal marriageable age diminish as female classmates and friends suddenly vanish from school and social activities, married off to older polygamists. Many young men were ostracized for one reason or another, leading to a group called the "lost boys."

The United Effort Plan (UEP) gave FLDS leaders total control over homes and property, and the Law of Placing gave them control over families and marriages. This form of dominion and compulsion was despised by early Church leaders like Joseph Smith, who delineated the results of such behavior: "The heavens withdraw themselves; the Spirit of the Lord is grieved; and when it is withdrawn, Amen to the priesthood or the authority of that man" (D&C 121:37).

Through the mid-twentieth century in Short Creek, each individual Priesthood Council member had the power to decide who would marry whom without discussing the arrangements with other council members. Followers who desired new wives could obtain the approval and cooperation of any member of the Priesthood Council to seal their marriages. In time, factions and cliques formed aligning themselves with the various council members.

THE "ONE MAN" DOCTRINE

One significant disagreement arose regarding the question of *presiding* authority: "Was there one man who ruled the PRIESTHOOD (and the group) or did the entire Priesthood Council preside?" Lorin Woolley's teachings on the subject were completely ambiguous and could easily support either position. Leroy Johnson, the senior Priesthood Council member disagreed with Marion Hammond, who was next in seniority, and eventually dismissed him from the council. Subsequently, Hammond, with council member Alma Timpson, left Colorado City and established the "Second Ward," in due course building their own meetinghouse. It was dedicated on September 27, 1986, precisely one hundred years after the date described by Lorin Woolley when John Taylor ordained five men to continue plural marriage. Consequently, the town was named "Centennial Park City."

Rulon Jeffs with Wives

With the dismissal of Hammond, Rulon Jeffs was left as the next senior member and immediately took charge upon Johnson's 1986 death. Jeffs too believed in the "one man" leadership theory. Accordingly, he followed Johnson's pattern by not calling any new council members, contradicting the pattern set in the past by Lorin C. Woolley and John Y. Barlow. Other

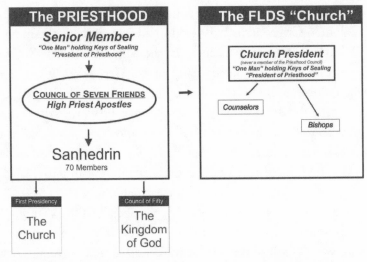

Woolley, Broadbent, Barlow, Musser - 1930s   FLDS Church after 1984

council members died so that by 1984, Rulon Jeffs ruled the FLDS Church and UEP alone and undisputed. A few counselors were called to assist, but they were not High Priest Apostles or marked to succeed Rulon Jeffs upon his death. Consequently, the religious organization had changed significantly since Woolley first described it.

In 2000, the combined population of Colorado City, Arizona, and Hildale, Utah, included over 5,200 people. Leroy S. Johnson had prophesied several times that the year 2000 would usher in the Millennium. Writer John Llewellyn penned: "On three occasions before Rulon Jeffs died, he called a select 2500 from his 10,000 members and instructed them to buy food and clothes and prepare to be lifted up. A plot of ground had actually been set aside designating the exact place of the gathering and expectant lifting. Before and after the lifting up, the faithful would need food and clothes. The utmost faithful purchased food in loyal anticipation, but the day before each gathering, Rulon called it off with the excuse that the Lord was giving them more time."[120]

Despite the primary headquarters of the FLDS Church in Colorado City, Rulon Jeffs lived in a large estate at the mouth of Little Cottonwood Canyon in the Salt Lake Valley. Several buildings accommodated many of his sixty-seven wives and their children. It also included a youth education facility called the "Alta Academy." Just prior to the year 2000, the Alta Academy and all the associated buildings and land were sold at a below-market rate. Then the entire population of the facility was transplanted to Colorado City, apparently in anticipation of some cataclysmic event that never materialized.

Rulon Jeffs passed away on September 7, 2002, creating a leadership vacuum in the FLDS Church. This lack of leadership was a result of the "one man" doctrine that prevented new

120. John R. Llewellyn, *Polygamy under Attack: From Tom Green to Brian David Mitchell* (Scottsdale, Ariz.: Agreka Books, 2004), 155.

council members from being called and a common belief that
Rulon Jeffs himself would be physically renewed and person-
ally deliver his priesthood keys back to Christ at the Second
Coming.

Failure of the expectations did not hamper the efforts of
Rulon's son Warren Jeffs from assuming the helm. He had been
positioning himself for a decade for the role, although he was
never ordained to any priesthood position that would legitimize his leadership. Through his own efforts, Warren became
the president of the UEP and had been his father's spokesman
for years. No other FLDS leader held the level of control that
he had acquired, and soon he was acknowledged as the new
leader of the FLDS Church.

Despite no reasonable claim to genuine sealing authority,
Warren Jeffs did not hunker down in a defensive posture there
in Colorado City. He soon excommunicated the sons of John
Y. Barlow and all other potential rivals, except Fred Jessop, who
died a year later. Next, he purchased land in Texas and over-

**Temple in Texas, constructed
under the direction of Warren Jeffs**

saw the building of a temple there. Temple building had never been a part of the FLDS tradition, except for one prophesied by Barlow and Musser to be constructed at Berry Knoll between Colorado City and Centennial Park.

The United States government also created a fortuitous distraction by issuing a warrant for Jeffs' arrest, ultimately landing him on the FBI's ten most wanted list. By diverting attention away from core issues regarding his seemingly indefensible claims to possessing genuine priesthood keys, Warren maintained solid control of the UEP fortunes and FLDS followers.

Jeffs was convicted in September 2007 on two counts of rape as an accomplice and given two five-years-to-life sentences. While imprisoned, he apparently experienced a change of heart and may have abdicated his position as leader. Rumors suggest that Wendell Nielsen, who was once described as one of Warren Jeffs' counselors, may have assumed the leadership role.

In April 2008, in response to a cell-phone call from a re-portedly underage and pregnant girl within the Eldorado com-pound, Texas Rangers invaded the grounds and even broke into the temple, searching for evidence of child abuse or other felonies. While it appeared state agents were not going to repeat the mistake of the state of Arizona in 1953, that of prosecut-ing the fathers for bigamy or polygamy, they were aggressive in taking over four hundred children into custody and assigning them to foster care. Law enforcement officers pledged to quick-ly identify the abusers and the abused through DNA testing and other methods. However, if the remaining mothers, chil-dren, and fathers, whose only crime is polygamy, are separated for more than a few weeks, it is probable that in years to come, the memory of this event will be retold in Texas with as much embarrassment as the 1953 raid has been recounted in Arizona during the past decades.

Concerning the FLDS members and the turmoil they have endured, it is likely that they will somehow continue the tradi-tion. The alternative is to acknowledge the deep confusion and disorder that exists regarding their claims to sealing authority. To concede that FLDS leaders lacked sealing priesthood is to label all their plural marriages as unauthorized. It would also devalue the intense suffering and inconveniences FLDS polyg-amy has exacted. Hope of eternal vindication and exaltation would be lost. Accordingly, relinquishing the FLDS tradition will probably be too difficult for most.

The Allred Group

With the split in Priesthood Council in 1952 and the death of Joseph W. Musser in 1954, Rulon C. Allred was left as the uncontested leader of those following the new council. Rulon continued to replace members of the Priesthood Council who died or apostatized. George W. Scott, Ormand F. Lavery, Marvin M. Jessop, J. Lamoine Jensen, George E. Maycock, John Whitman Ray, Morris Y. Jessop, and William H. Baird were called. Throughout the 1960s, the Allred Group membership expanded through new converts and childbirths (which were plentiful). Plural marriages, always performed by members of the Priesthood Council, might take place in a home, a church, a meadow, high in the surrounding mountains, or at a sacred altar. They eventually incorporated themselves as the Apostolic United Brethren Church, or AUB for short.

Rulon Allred decided in 1961 to purchase 640 acres of ranch land in the Bitterroot Mountains of Montana, with the intent of establishing a united order there. In 1983, it was incorporated as the city of Pinesdale, located close to Hamilton and Missoula. By 1973, more than 400 fundamentalists called it home, increasing to over 800 persons and 250 families in 1998. Besides a large

Rulon C. Allred

The ten members of the AUB Council of Seven Friends or Priesthood Council in 1990. Back left: Orman Lavery, Owen A. Allred, Marvin, Allred, Joseph Thompson, and Bill Baird. Front left: Lynn Thompson, George Maycock (excommunicated 1998) J. LaMoine Jenson (current leader), Marvin Jessop, and Morris Jessop

concentration in the Salt Lake City area, today adherents may be found in several locations in central and southern Utah, including Rocky Ridge and Cedar City. In 1970, the number of AUB members was close to 2,500 expanding to over 6,000 by the year 2000.

In contrast to earlier leaders, Rulon Allred did not consider himself and his Priesthood Council to be superior to The Church of Jesus Christ of Latter-day Saints and its leadership. He taught: "[We] are not in a position to dictate to the Church, or to presume that we preside over President David O. McKay [then President of the Church]… or that we can in any way dictate the affairs of the Church."[121] He further explained: "We are functioning within the spiritual confines of the Church but

121. Rulon Allred, discourse given on November 16, 1966, as quoted in Gilbert Fulton, *Gems,* 3 vols. (Salt Lake City: Gems Publishing, 1967), 1:4.

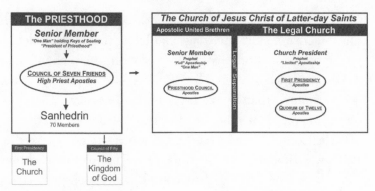

Woolley, Broadbent, Barlow, Musser - 1930s   The AUB Under Rulon Allred

we are definitely outside of its legal organization."[122] As Rulon Allred described it, his organization and its relationship with the Church seemed to contradict the teaching of Lorin Woolley in the early 1930s.

Rulon Allred assured his followers that he held the necessary priesthood authority to perform valid plural marriages. Ironically, he also taught that the polygamists did not need to serve as missionaries or to perform temple work for the dead. LDS theology teaches that the "one" man who holds the keys of sealing also controls all other priesthood keys (see D&C 128:11, 28:7, 81:2, 110:11–12, 132:7). Importantly for that "one" man, receiving that *fullness of the priesthood keys* also includes receiving a *fullness of priesthood responsibilities*. Equally important, receiving *limited priesthood keys* includes receiving *limited priesthood responsibilities*. For example, the president of the deacons quorum has both limited authority (keys) and limited responsibility.

Despite the obvious inconsistency, Mormon fundamentalist leaders today generally claim to have received *all* priesthood keys (which are required to perform eternal marriages of any kind whether polygamous or monogamous). Yet they claim to

122. Rulon C. Allred, *Treasures of Knowledge: Selected Discourses and Excerpts from Talks,* 2 vols. (Hamilton, Mont.: Bitterroot Publishing, 1981) 2:13.

have received only *limited* priesthood responsibilities, specifically, practicing plural marriage and living the united order.

Competition and disagreements with the LeBarons in Mexico, with whom Allred lived in 1947–48, expanded in the 1950s so much that Rulon felt a need to respond. He chose John Butchreit, a member of the 1952 Priesthood Council, to visit Mexico in 1956 and set the LeBarons straight. Nevertheless, it was Butchreit who became converted to the teachings of the LeBarons, joining their church and seeking proselytes to their group. Eventually the conflict would escalate until in 1977, the psychopathic Ervil sent a hit team to shoot Rulon dead.

Rulon Allred's brother Owen succeeded his brother as leader of the AUB. One of Owen's sons observed that: "Owen Allred never wanted the responsibility of leading the 5,000 member church . . . [but] shouldered the responsibility and did the best he could."[123] Owen passed away February 14, 2005. During the one and a half years prior to his death: "He wanted to go. I don't think that one single day passed by that he didn't say he wanted to go home."[124] J. LaMoine Jenson succeeded Own Allred as the head of the AUB by appointment. Although other council members were more senior, Own Allred had designated Jenson to fill his place upon his death, and, apparently, the other council members and AUB followers concurred.

123. Carl Allred, quoted in Leigh Dethman, "1300 Pay Respects to Owen Allred," *Deseret Morning News,* February 20, 2005, B-1.
124. Ibid., B-2.

The Kingstons

During the 1920s, hundreds of dissenters from the LDS Church coalesced into specific groups across the Wasatch Front. Among the participants was Charles W. Kingston. Charles Zitting (one of Lorin C. Woolley's High Priest Apostles) introduced Kingston to plural marriage, causing Kingston to be cut off from the Church in 1929. Two weeks after is excommunication, Kingston had a dream wherein he believed he was visited by Jesus Christ and God the Father. He interpreted his dream to mean that God approved of his leaving the Church. While his children and wife initially resisted his new religious position, they eventually joined him in asking their names to be removed from LDS Church records.

While Charles W. Kingston was the first to oppose the Church, the primary mover in the Kingston Group was his son Elden. Elden theorized that living the law of consecration was still required, and he set forth to establish his own united order organization. While engaged in that enterprise, he reportedly received an angelic visitation. His father wrote:

> Brother Elden received a new covenant up on the top of the highest mountain that is east of Bountiful, Utah. When the Lord chose Brother Elden through which to send this new covenant, all other covenants were thereby dissolved. This means all other covenants were of no effect through which source they can. (The Church lost its authority to give covenants.) . . . Satan

> will try to stop the power of the Lord and that power is
> where the Lord has given his covenant of consecration
> and that is: to the Davis County Co-op of Bountiful,
> Utah. It is the power of God through the law or cove-
> nant of consecration given to Brother Elden in 1935.[125]
>
> The Church . . . lost the priesthood which had come
> down to them from the Prophet Joseph Smith. . . .
> Brother Elden had received a new dispensation of the
> gospel of Jesus Christ. . . . [The Lord] had to institute
> another New and Everlasting Covenant which he gave
> to another 25 year old boy on the highest mountain east
> of Bountiful on the first day of the year, 1935. . . . Elden
> received the covenant of consecration and also the plan
> of temporal salvation.[126]

Accordingly, Elden became the first prophet of the Kingston Group and established the Davis County Cooperative

Society. The Co-op members practiced
plural marriage and abided by a rigid hierarchy of leadership and deference.

Precisely where Elden obtained valid
priesthood authority is a matter of dis-
pute. Elden's father related that Elden
told him that was ordained by J. Leslie
Broadbent (Lorin Woolley's successor)
in 1934, although precisely what that ordination represented is unclear. Kingston members today generally claim that

Elden Kingston

keys were received anew from heavenly
messengers directly to Elden in 1935, although it appears he
left no formal testimony to that effect. LDS scripture teaches
that "in the mouth of two or three witnesses shall every word
be established" (D&C 6:28; 2 Cor. 13:1). Elden's solo expe-

125. Charles William Kingston, "Autobiography," 23–24; spelling and
punctuation standardized. Photocopy in author's possession.
126. Ibid., 141–42.

rience of receiving the priesthood keys and authority is truly singular and contrasts the pattern previously given by the Lord for important priesthood conferrals that require more than one witness.

Believing that Elden received lost priesthood keys in 1935 also seems to contradict an 1837 scripture given to Joseph Smith stating that the priesthood had then (in 1837) been restored "for the last time": "For unto you, the Twelve, and those, the First Presidency, who are appointed with you to be your counselors and your leaders, is the power of this priesthood given, for the last days and for the last time, in the which is the dispensation of the fulness of times (D&C 112:30; see also D&C 27:13). According to Kingston teachings, this scripture should not be taken too literally, and all of the efforts commenced through Joseph Smith came to a dead halt in 1934, thereby necessitating Elden Kingston to initiate a new dispensation. Elden clearly claimed to hold the priesthood keys, saying, "I have those keys of power."[127]

The Kingston's claim that Elden received a new dispensation is problematic in another way. The word "dispensation" refers to two processes. First, the truth and the priesthood keys are *dispensed* from heaven to a prophet on earth. Second, that prophet organizes his followers into missionary forces that *dispense* the truth to all the world, utilizing the priesthood to perform saving ordinances. If somehow a new dispensation came through Elden Kingston in 1935, it was stillborn, because it was never dispensed to God's children. The Kingston Group stopped proselytizing new converts when the cooperative became successful, and today they perform no missionary work of any kind.

Through diligent money management and hard work, the

---

127. Charles Elden Kingston discourse, "1940 New Years Meeting, 8:40 a.m. to 12:30 a.m.", 11; emphasis in original. Unpublished; copy of typescript in author's possession.

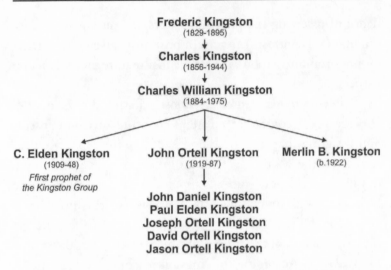

Davis County Cooperative Society became very financially successful. In the 1940s and 50s, Kingston followers designed and wore unique outer garments, the wearing of which led other people to refer to them as "blue-coats." Men and boys wore a blue coverall-type suit tied with strings, while women and girls wore plain blue dresses. As a symbol of their renunciation of worldly goods, the outer clothing contained no pockets in which possessions could be carried, although later an inside pocket was provided for the sanitary measure of carrying a handkerchief. All went bareheaded and barefoot.

Elden passed away from cancer in 1948 and was succeeded by his brother John Ortell Kingston (commonly known as Ortell). During the 1940s, Ortell worked on a dairy farm owned by the Co-op at Woodscross, Davis County, Utah, where he reportedly developed theories on genetics, theories he later decided could be used to purify his own family pedigree. Connie Rugg, one of Ortell's plural wives remembered: "[Ortell Kingston] experimented inbreeding with his cattle and then he turned to his children."[128] Ortell desired to perfect his own bloodline

128. Andrea Moore-Emmett, *God's Brothel* (San Francisco: Pince-Nez, 2004), 88.

and implemented practices that encouraged marriages of close relatives. Those unions fell within Utah's consanguinity restrictions and, if discovered, would be considered incestuous under the laws of the state. Several charges of incest would eventually be leveled against various Kingston members.

**In the 1940s, members of the
Co-op wore blue bib overalls**

Over the past decades, the Kingston Group has maintained extreme secrecy while developing an extensive cooperative system, with wealth in at least 50 corporations in Utah and scattered across the West. Assets are generally estimated to be in the range of $200 million, although one Colorado competitor gave an even more stratospheric guess, pegging the clan's wealth at $11 billion. Unfortunately, there are also numerous reports of members who lived in squalor in order to advance the monetary gains of the Co-op. Supposedly, these sacrifices are part of the united order. However, the law of consecration has a purpose beyond self-sacrifice.

The Doctrine and Covenants admonishes the Saints to "look to the poor and the needy, and administer to their re-

Ortel Kingston

lief that they shall not suffer" (D&C 38:35). We specifically read that the law of consecration is designed "to administer to the poor and the needy" (D&C 42:35). "And it is my purpose to provide for my saints, for all things are mine. But it must needs be done in mine own way; and behold this is the way that I, the Lord, have decreed to provide for my saints, that the poor shall be exalted, in that the rich are made low" (D&C 104:16).

A brief review of the accomplishments of the Co-op produces an impressive spreadsheet with assets in excess of $200 million. But it is unclear how such assets are exalting the poor or making the rich low. In fact, the leaders of the Co-op just seem to be getting richer and the poor get essentially ignored. It may be that the Co-op is trying to help the poor in some anonymous way, but I have seen no evidence of it. In addition, placing the law of consecration at the pinnacle of divine laws is inconsistent with scripture and restoration history. We recall that Joseph Smith made no effort to implement the law of consecration while in Nauvoo (see D&C 105:34). Brigham Young waited until 1868, twenty-one years after arriving in Utah, to actively promote it, and John Taylor ceased emphasizing it shortly after becoming President of the Church.

Some Kingston followers might justify their financial conglomerate by comparing it to the wealthy Church of Jesus Christ of Latter-day Saints. It is true that the LDS Church has collected tithes and offerings in the millions of dollars over the past decades. But rather than amassing a fortune for the sake of accumulating wealth or to simply sustain a few selected leaders, donations flow into the Church coffers and out again to provide financial support for the accomplishment of the Church's responsibilities regarding missionary work, temple work, and providing for physical welfare needs.

Upon Ortell's death in 1987, leadership passed to his son Paul Elden Kingston. Paul continued to practice his father's ideas regarding intra-family marriages. Daughters of men in the Co-op would be married off at young ages. LuAnn Kingston, a former member of the clan who in 1995 at age fifteen was forced to marry her first cousin, shared: "The joke used to be that if you weren't married by 17, you were an old maid."[129]

Within the Kingston Group, the primary polygamists are the immediate Kingston family and heirs. Reportedly, Paul and his brother each have dozens of wives and hundreds of children. One brother, John Daniel Kingston, was taken to court for neglecting this children. When asked to name his offspring by plural wife Mattingly Foster, Kingston came up with about five names before faltering, saying he was "very nervous." After viewing a list of the children, he then attempted to name them but once more fell short—prompting the judge to supply the final child's name for him. Kingston was able to name only nine of his thirteen children by a second woman, Rachael Ann Kingston. "Sounds like I left a few out," he said after being reminded of how many children he had fathered in that family.[130]

The Kingstons represent an intriguing branch on the Mormon fundamentalist tree. While they affirm that they now carry the torch first lit by Joseph Smith, their agenda focuses only on plural marriage and their own brand of united order. The Prophet Joseph's priorities of missionary work, temple ordinances, proxy work for the dead, and feeding the poor appear to have been lost somewhere. Early persecution seems to have

129. Michael Janofsky, "Young Brides Stir New Outcry on Utah Polygamy," *New York Times*, February 27, 2003, Late Edition—Final Section A-1.

130. Brooke Adams, *Salt Lake Tribune*, May 22, 2004.

conditioned Kingston leaders to maintain the utmost secrecy, but third generation officers seem to use ignorance as a tool to enhance control of their followers, especially of women. With the dawn of the twenty-first century, lawsuits and education among Kingston followers would combine to create new obstacles, as leaders perpetuate this financial-spiritual hybrid organization.

The LeBarons

The LeBaron polygamists broke away from other Mormon fundamentalists in 1955. Prior to that time, they had loosely associated with John Y. Barlow and later Rulon Allred. LeBaron theology is distinct from all other fundamentalist factions in that they believe that the "one" man holding the keys of sealing does so by virtue of a priesthood office unheard of prior to 1955, the office called "the Right of the Firstborn."

The theology is rather complex, but asserts that "the Right of the Firstborn" presides over all priesthood and over the church patriarch, who in turn presides over the First Presidency.

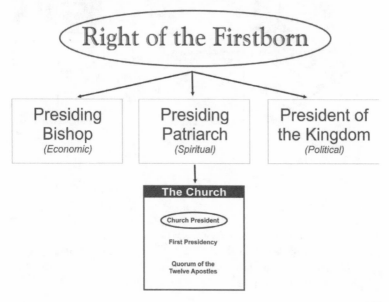

The term is found in Abraham 1:2–3 where Abraham writes: "I became a rightful heir, a High Priest, holding the right belonging to the fathers. It was conferred upon me from the fathers; it came down from the fathers, from the beginning of time, yea, even from the beginning, or before the foundation of the earth, down to the present time, even *the right of the first-born*, or the first man, who is Adam, or first father, through the fathers unto me" (italics added). According to LeBaron teachings, the "Right of the Firstborn" means "the right to stand in the stead of the firstborn in His absence; the firstborn being Christ."[131]

Reportedly the first man to hold this position in this dispensation was Joseph Smith. This office was then to pass to "his posterity after him" based upon a novel interpretation of a scripture talking about the building of the Nauvoo House—D&C 124:56–60. Regardless, the LeBarons hold that none of Joseph Smith's posterity actually received the office, but instead it went to Benjamin F. Johnson, who they allege was an

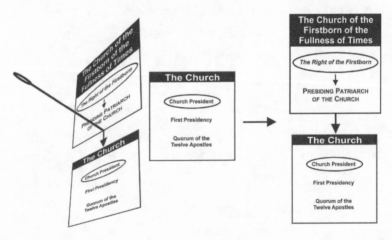

---

131. Ervil LeBaron, *Priesthood Expounded* (Buenaventura, Chihuahua, Mexico, 1956), 8:19. (Divided into Section and Verse by Thomas J. Liddiard March 1988.) Contrast with Abraham 1:3, which indicates that the "Right of the Firstborn" refers to Adam.

"adopted son." There is no evidence that Johnson was adopted by the Prophet, or that he ever believed himself in possession of such a lofty office and responsibility.

Like the Woolley fundamentalists discussed earlier, it appears that LeBaron fundamentalists have simply superimposed their ideas on the restored Church.

At any rate, LeBaron fundamentalists assumed that shortly before Benjamin F. Johnson's death on November 18, 1905, he bypassed all eighteen of his own sons who were then alive in order to ordain one of his one hundred and five grandsons also living at that time. That chosen grandson was reportedly A. Dayer LeBaron. Ervil LeBaron penned: "Shortly before the death of Benjamin F. Johnson, he called his grandson, Alma Dayer LeBaron Sr. . . . He gave him many instructions and said to him: When I die, my mantle will fall upon you."[132]

Curiously, Dayer LeBaron left no testimony that he possessed any special priesthood authority. Regardless, sometime before his death, LeBaron polygamists believe he gave his keys to one of his sons. Ben seems to have the most legitimate claim because he was the firstborn. Reportedly he once stopped traffic in downtown Salt Lake City while he did two hundred push-ups to prove that he was the "one mighty and strong" (from D&C 85:7). Ben spent most of his life battling mental illness.

Other accounts discussing Dayer's priesthood keys written years after his death assert that they were given to Joel. Similarly, Ross Welsey claimed that he was ordained by his father Dayer LeBaron some months prior to his father's death. Later both Ervil and Verlan would assume to hold the described office of the "Right of the Firstborn," although years before Verlan LeBaron had approached Rulon C. Allred to perform his sealing to a plural wife. Sons Alma, Floren, and David never claimed their father's alleged authority.

---

132. Ibid., 19:24.

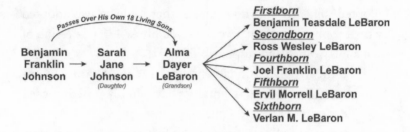

THREE LEBARON CHURCHES

Sometime in the early 1950s, Joel LeBaron resorted to the mountains, seeking answers to specific prayers regarding the "one mighty and strong" mentioned in D&C 85:7. In response, he described receiving a visitation from heavenly messengers: "They talked to me as plain as you and I are talking together. I now know the exact pattern to be used in setting the house of God in order."[133] In August of 1955, Joel visited Salt Lake City and, accompanied by his brothers Ross and Floren, proceeded to organize his own church, "The Church of the Firstborn of the Fulness of Times."

Once the church was organized on September 21, 1955, baptisms and confirmations followed that very same day. The new church boasted three members, but its leaders expected many more to soon join. The LeBaron teachings suggest that The Church of Jesus Christ of Latter-day Saints "was established to prepare the saints for membership in the Church of the Firstborn."[134] At the urging of his brother Floren, Joel sought a secluded corner in a canyon above Salt Lake City. Then prayerfully seeking a confirmation of his calling, he reported receiving a "personal visitation from no less than nineteen prophets, including Abraham, Moses, Christ, and Joseph Smith."

Within months of the organization of the Church of the Firstborn of the Fulness of Times, disagreements arose causing Joel and

133. Verlan LeBaron, *The LeBaron Story* (Lubbock, Tex.: Keels and Company, 1981), 34–35.
134. Fred C. Collier, *The Church of the Firstborn and the Holy Order of God* (Salt Lake City: Colliers, 1977), 2.

LeBaron Brothers, Ervil, Joel, Verlan, Alma, and Floren

Ross to part ways. On December 1, 1955, Ross Wesley LeBaron incorporated his own church calling it simply "The Church of the Firstborn." During the ensuing decades, Ross remained in Utah and quietly promoted his own church, cultivating a small group of followers. When asked in an interview on July 25, 1959, concerning his priesthood authority, Ross stated that he was "ordained by his father in March, 1950, and that Joseph W. Musser confirmed the patriarchal Priesthood of Dayer LeBaron the same day."[135]

Initially Ervil LeBaron was one of Joel's greatest disciples, however, by mid-May 1971, Ervil claimed his own revelation telling him to start his own church, and he organized the "Church of the Lamb of God." Subsequently he and Dan Jordan were excommunicated from Joel's church. The family matriarch, Maud LeBaron, wrote a letter to Ervil stating: "Your father came to my bedside last week and asked me to help remove the sorrowful condition," but even her intervention was ineffective is stemming the tide of Ervil's darkening intentions.

---

135. Quoted in Lyle O. Wright, "Origins and Development of the Church of the Firstborn," (master's thesis, Brigham Young University, 1963), 175, 250. For his brother's differing view, see LeBaron, *The LeBaron Story,* 64.

CHURCH	LEADER	DATE ORGANIZED
The Church of the Firstborn of the Fulness of Times	Joel LeBaron*	September 21, 1955
The Church of the Firstborn	Ross Wesley LeBaron	December 1, 1955
The Church of the Lamb of God	Ervil LeBaron	May 20, 1971

* Initially presided over by Joel LeBaron. At Joel's death, Verlan LeBaron became the new leader.

Disputations between the brothers led Ervil to seek Joel's death, perpetrated by Dan Jordan on August 20, 1972. Verlan was next in Ervil's cross hairs, but after several years and multiple failed attempts to kill him, Ervil concocted an

Ervil in Mexican Prison

elaborate plan. He demanded that Rulon Allred tithe to him, and when Rulon refused, Ervil dispatched two of his young wives to shoot Allred in his doctor's office. Ervil was certain that Verlan would attend Allred's funeral, and there Ervil's assassins could gun him down. Allred was killed, and Verlan did attend the funeral, but the media and law enforcement officers were too thick and his hit men bolted. Ervil was extradited to Utah and convicted of Rulon Allred's murder, dying in prison in 1981.

Besides the lethal drama accompanying much of the LeBaron history, significant problems exist in their theology. The essentially "made-to-order" design of the line of priesthood au-

thority proclaimed by LeBaron factions might seem to legitimize their claims. A closer look demonstrates that the offices
and teachings greatly contrast Joseph Smith's revelations and
instructions. Foremost, the Lord tells us twice in section 132:
"My house is a house of order" (D&C 132:8, 18), and order is
lacking. The theological discrepancies seem insurmountable to
objective reviewers.

Independents and other Mormon Fundamentalists

Besides the groups addressed above, several other notable Mormon fundamentalists deserve mention.

Lorin C. Woolley	New Dispensation	"Independents"	Other
• FLDS - Colorado City • AUB - Allred Group • Kingston?	• Kingston? • TLC - Harmston	• Ogden Kraut • Tom Green • Royston Potter • Singer - Swapp	• Alex Joseph • Laffertys • Brian David Mitchell

JAMES T. HARMSTON AND
THE TRUE AND LIVING CHURCH

James D. Harmston and his wife were active members of the LDS Church but were unhappy with certain practices and teachings. They broke away from the Church in the 1980s, dedicating a special room in their home to carry out priesthood functions Church members reserve for holy temples. In response to their prayers, they reported that the heavens were opened, and they received visits from divine messengers including the Father and the Son. Specifically, on November 25, 1990, Enoch, Noah, Abraham, and Moses appeared to Harmston to bestow priesthood keys they had reportedly seized from errant LDS Church leaders.

Harmston and his wife immediately established their own "True and Living Church of Jesus Christ of Saints of the Last Days" (TLC) with Harmston as president, prophet, seer, and revelator. Located at Manti, Utah, they gathered several hundred followers and in 1997 increased their numbers further through the development of a sophisticated website.

With plural marriage as an active tenet of the TLC, Harmston accumulated eight wives by 1998, mostly from other fundamentalist groups.

One unique doctrine of the TLC is "multiple mortal probations" or MMPs. Similar in some ways to reincarnation (of Buddhist and Hindu persuasion), Harmston has admitted that he is in fact Joseph Smith, Isaiah, King Arthur, and, reportedly after viewing the movie *Braveheart*, he suddenly remembered he had also previously lived as William Wallace. Members who receive a patriarchal blessing from the church patriarch are commonly told of their former mortal lives as well as their current probation.

Reportedly, Harmston's first wife Elaine is a necromancer. "She has a special, pink room with an alter where she communicates with the dead ancestors of the TLC members to see if the dead would like to be proxy-baptized into the TLC."[136]

While the group reported approximately 500 members in 2002, it appears their numbers have dwindled due to unfulfilled prophesies and dissatisfaction with Harmston's leadership.

ALEX JOSEPH AND
THE CONFEDERATE NATIONS OF ISRAEL

Alex Joseph was one of the more colorful characters in Mormon fundamentalism. He joined the LDS Church in 1955

---

136. John R. Llewellyn, *Polygamy under Attack: From Tom Green to Brian David Mitchell* (Scottsdale, Ariz.: Agreka Books, 2004), 66.

at age twenty-nine, and then five years later left, aligning himself with the Allred Group. Moving to Pinesdale, Montana, he joined the polygamist colony there. With his charisma and intelligence, he successfully convinced several coeds from the nearby University of Montana to become his plural wives, including two Catholics, a Methodist, and a Presbyterian. Their parents were outraged, requiring Rulon Allred to call Alex to repentance. Allred pointed out that Joseph's marriages were performed without the approval of the Priesthood Council. In response, Alex said: "You did it, Rulon, and now I'm following your example." He was asked to leave the Montana settlement three years after moving there.

Following his own brand of Christian ideals including polygamy, Alex Joseph moved himself and his families to Glen Canyon City in Kane County, Utah, calling it Big Water and served as its first mayor. Together with his families and followers, Joseph built a cultural center for the community that was large enough to accommodate several hundred people with apartments for each of his wives, naming it Long Haul.

Prior to his death, Joseph served as a politician, Marine, policeman, firefighter, mail carrier, car salesman, accountant, author of many books, and health food producer. He died leaving seven wives, twenty-one children, and twenty-three grandchildren.

RON AND DAN LAFFERTY

Ron and Dan Lafferty grew up in a strict LDS family with an authoritarian father of six boys. Educated as a chiropractor, Dan investigated Mormon fundamentalist teachings shortly after he was first married and quickly shared his beliefs with Ron. Worried that Ron might give their oldest daughter away into a polygamous marriage and with the encouragement of sister-in-law Brenda Wright Lafferty (wife of the youngest brother Allen), Ron's wife divorced him.

In response, Ron received a revelation that Brenda and her fifteen-month-old child should be killed. Ron and Dan carried out the gruesome murders in 1984 and were later convicted, with Ron sentenced to death (currently on death row) and Dan serving a life prison sentence.

BRIAN DAVID MITCHELL

In the early 1990s, Brian David Mitchell lived as an active member of The Church of Jesus Christ of Latter-day Saints and served as a temple worker. Enticed by marginal religious teachings that criticized orthodox medical care, he stopped taking his medication prescribed for mental instability. Shortly thereafter, he quit his job, changed his name to Immanuel David Isaiah, donned a long robe and with his wife, Wanda Barzee, set forth to wander the country, panhandling for support.

In consequence of teaching his eccentric views to others, he was excommunicated from the LDS Church in November 2001. The following April, Mitchell compiled a twenty-seven-page manifesto that included his own revelations and beliefs. Speaking for God, one revelation dated February 9, 2002 stated: "I have raised up my servant Immanuel David Isaiah, even my righteous right hand, to be a light and a covenant to my people—to all those who will repent and come unto me, for in my servant, Immanuel David Isaiah, is the fullness of the gospel, which I, the Lord brought forth out of obscurity and out of darkness through my servant Joseph Smith, Jr."[137]

Among Mitchell's writings is a manifesto that promotes the law of consecration and plural marriage. One revelation addressed to "Hepzibah," Mitchell's wife Barzee, states: "Wherefore, Hepzibah, my most cherished angel, thou wilt take into thy heart and home seven sisters. . . . And thou shalt take into thy heart and home seven times seven sisters, to love and care

---

137. Brian David Mitchell, "The Book of Immanuel David Isaiah," (written April 6, 2002), 1; photocopy in author's possession.

for; forty-nine precious jewels in thy crown, and thou art the jubilee of them all, first and last."[138]

This revelation, though written after Elizabeth Smart was abducted, reflects the motives that undoubtedly prompted Mitchell and Barzee to kidnap Smart on June 5, 2002. Elizabeth was to be one of the "forty-nine precious jewels" that were suppose to eventually wed Brian David Mitchell.

INDEPENDENTS

As with all fundamentalists groups, significant numbers also leave the flock each year. For example, Rulon Allred often sorrowed that men would leave his priesthood group and function independent of his authority and the Priesthood Council's guidance. "We find men in the Priesthood who grow so self-confident in their own ability to cope with all situations that they no longer need the direction of their file leaders in anything. They no longer attend their Priesthood meetings. They become independent."[139] Prominent names among this group are Ogden Kraut, Tom Green, Royston Potter, and John Singer.

"Independent" Mormon fundamentalists approach the need for legitimate sealing authority in a number of creative ways. Many ignore the issue, feeling that their own personal revelations and sincerity will overcome the lack of genuine authority. Others seem willing to believe the claims of just about any man who states he possesses sealing keys, without checking their line of authority too closely. Some polygamists report elaborate dreams and visions wherein they are given keys on a ring or ordinations from angelic messengers. Thereafter they feel justified to seal marriages including their own.

138. Ibid., 23.
139. Rulon C. Allred, *Treasures of Knowledge: Selected Discourses and Excerpts from Talks,* 2 vols. (Hamilton, Mont.: Bitterroot Publishing, 1981), 2:47.

Doctrinal Issues

Over the years since 1904, significant doctrinal differences have emerged between the Mormon fundamentalists and The Church of Jesus Christ of Latter-day Saints. Fundamentalists embrace a much more novel, if not extreme interpretation of several theological tenets. The distinctions are briefly discussed below. (A more in-depth discussion can be found at www.mormonfundamentalism.com.)

1. *Mormon fundamentalists believe that suspending the practice of plural marriage is changing a priesthood ordinance.*

2. *Mormon fundamentalists embrace a unique interpretation of an 1886 revelation given to President John Taylor.*

3. *Mormon fundamentalists believe that The Church of Jesus Christ of Latter-day Saints is the "house of God" that the "one mighty and strong" (mentioned in D&C 85:7) will "set in order."*

4. *Mormon fundamentalists believe that only certain words can be used to confer priesthood authority during ordinations and that any variation results in a defection ordination.*

5. *Mormon fundamentalists seem to be guided by a different spirit than that followed by LDS Church members.*

6. *Section 132 of the Doctrine and Covenants emphasizes the importance of proper priesthood authority in sealing eternal marriage (monogamous or polygamous), which is sometimes ignored by modern polygamists.*

*1. Mormon fundamentalists believe that suspending the practice
of plural marriage is changing a priesthood ordinance.*

Joseph Smith taught: "Where there is no change of priesthood, there is no change of ordinances."[140] Modern polygamists
sometimes assert that Church leaders changed the ordinance
of plural marriage by discontinuing its practice in 1904, and
therefore they also changed the priesthood. Such allegations
prompt important questions for Latter-day Saints: Is plural
marriage an ordinance? Are there "keys to plural marriage" as
some fundamentalists have claimed?

Throughout the scriptures and the teachings of Joseph
Smith, Brigham Young, and other Church leaders, there are
apparently no references to *keys of plural marriage* or an *ordinance of plural marriage*. In LDS theology, however, there are
keys of sealing and the *ordinance of sealing* allowing a man and a
woman to be married eternally. President John Taylor testified
in 1884 that there is "no distinction" between the authority
used to seal a monogamist marriage verses a polygamist marriage.[141] Accordingly, *plural marriage itself is not an ordinance. It
is the repetition of an ordinance*, the ordinance of sealing.

Church leaders have consistently taught that the same keys
are used to seal either a monogamist or a polygamist marriage.
History shows that the sealing keys have been continually ex-
ercised by Presidents of the Church from 1841 to the present
day in ceremonies that seal a man and a woman in eternal
marriage. Prior to 1904, the man involved in a new sealing
may have been previously sealed to other living women, but the
ceremony itself would not have revealed that fact. Currently,
the sealing authority is used only for marriages where the man
has no living spouse.

---

140. Joseph Fielding Smith, comp., *Teachings of the Prophet Joseph Smith*
(Salt Lake City: Deseret Book, 1976), 308.
141. Testimony given at the trial of Rudger Clawson, *Deseret Evening
News*, October 18, 1884.

Latter-day Saints assert that the ordinance of eternal sealing has not been changed in any way, though its application has been limited to monogamous living couples through the "one" holding the keys. In contrast, most Mormon fundamentalists believe polygamous marriages must continue to be performed or the authority to solemnize them will be lost.

2. Mormon fundamentalists embrace a unique interpretation of an 1886 revelation to President John Taylor.

In the decades after the Church was organized, several Church Presidents besides Joseph Smith, received revelations that were never canonized or included in the Doctrine and Covenants. One such revelation was written by President John Taylor on Monday, September 27, 1886. While some observers have questioned its authenticity, it appears the document is genuine. It reads:

> September 27, 1886
>
> My son John: You have asked me concerning the New and Everlasting Covenant and how far it is binding upon my people.
>
> Thus saith the Lord All commandments that I give must be obeyed by those calling themselves by my name unless they are revoked by me or by my authority and how can I revoke an everlasting covenant.
>
> For I the Lord am everlasting and my covenants cannot be abrogated nor done away with; but they stand forever.
>
> Have I not given my word in great plainness on this subject?
>
> Yet have not great numbers of my people been negligent in the observance of my law and the keeping of my commandment, and yet have I borne with them these many years and this because of their weakness because of the perilous times. And furthermore it is more pleasing to me that men should use their free agency in regard to these matters.

> Nevertheless I the Lord do not change and my word and my covenants and my law do not.
>
> And as I have heretofore said by my servant Joseph all those who would enter into my glory must and shall obey my law.
>
> And have I not commanded men that if they were Abraham's seed and would enter into my glory they must do the works of Abraham.
>
> I have not revoked this law nor will I for it is everlasting and those who will enter into my glory must obey the conditions thereof, even so Amen.[142]

We do not know the precise question that prompted this revelation to President Taylor, though it apparently involved the new and everlasting covenant. Nor do we understand how he personally responded to it. It does not appear that he ever discussed the existence of the revelation or its significance with other Church members prior to his passing on July 25, 1887. The paper upon which this revelation was written was found among John Taylor's personal effects by his son, apostle John W. Taylor, sometime after his father's death. John W. Taylor reported that he subsequently shared it with a few friends.

Mormon fundamentalists usually believe that this revelation was given during an eight-hour meeting held on September 27, 1886, wherein President John Taylor floated above the floor as he put thirteen Church members under covenant to continue plural marriage independent of the Church if needed. Also, reportedly five copies of the revelation were made. None of the described

John Taylor

142. Fred C. Collier, *Unpublished Revelations of the prophets and presidents of The Church of Jesus Christ of Latter-day Saints*, 2nd ed., 2 vols. (Salt Lake City: Collier's Publishing, 1979–present), 1:88.

copies has ever been seen or ever referred to since that day. Importantly, available evidence contradicts that a meeting was held that day or that John Taylor (or the other participants listed by Woolley) were ever involved with such a remarkable gathering.

Of all the uncanonized revelations received by John Taylor and other Church Presidents, none would become more controversial than this one. Post-1904 polygamists would become convinced that somewhere within its paragraphs, God was stating that plural marriage could never be suspended.

One Mormon fundamentalist writer summed up the general interpretation held even by polygamists today: "Here the Lord very clearly and definitely says, that in order to enter into His glory, men MUST live the law of plural marriage. He makes no exceptions. There are no 'ifs' nor 'ands' about it. 'All those who would enter into my glory MUST and SHALL obey my law.' And 'my law,' as the Lord was treating it, is the law of plural marriage" (emphasis in original).[143]

Another fundamentalist author penned: "In the revelation to John Taylor, dated September 27, 1886, the Lord said that he had not, could not and would not revoke the Law of Abraham which is Plural Marriage. . . . The Lord has commanded in no uncertain terms that we must obey this law of Celestial Marriage, that is plural marriage, in order to obtain exaltation."[144]

Similarly, as early as the 1920s, polygamists would teach that the *commandments* referred to in this 1886 revelation, as well as the *conditions* of the law (which must be obeyed), all point to plural marriage. Some Mormon fundamentalists would also suggest that the new and everlasting covenant men-

---

143. Joseph Musser, "Evidences and Reconciliations," *Truth* 6 (December 1940) 158.
144. Lynn L. Bishop, *The 1886 Visitations of Jesus Christ and Joseph Smith to John Taylor: the Centerville Meetings* (Salt Lake City: Latter-day Publications, 1998), 63.

tioned here is singly plural marriage. In addition, they would affirm that Abraham was a polygamist and so to "do the *works of Abraham*" would require the practice of plural marriage.

In contrast, Church scholars believe that the Mormon fundamentalist interpretation is unjustified, noting that the words employed do not naturally convey the interpretation promoted by polygamist writers. LDS scriptorians generally conclude that the *law, covenants, conditions, commandments,* and *works of Abraham* allude to much broader gospel principles than exclusively plural marriage.

The 1886 revelation speaks of a "law" that cannot be "revoked." LDS scriptures contain no reference to a "law of plural marriage," nor does it appear that Joseph Smith, Brigham Young, or John Taylor ever mentioned it. However, the "law of *celestial* marriage" is discussed. Three years prior to receiving this revelation, President Taylor distinguished between the *law of celestial marriage* and the *principle of plural marriage* saying: "[God] has told us about our wives and our children being sealed to us, that we might have a claim on them in eternity. He has revealed unto us the *Law* of Celestial Marriage, associated with which is the *principle* of plural marriage."[145] Church teachings support that plural marriage itself is most accurately described as a "principle" rather than a *law.*

It also appears that the *law* mentioned in the 1886 revelation is the same *law* discussed in section 132 of the Doctrine and Covenants. Church members maintain that verses nineteen and twenty of that section describe how the *law* is fulfilled as "*a man* marries *a wife*" by proper authority, with promises of exaltation extended to monogamist couples who are properly sealed and live worthily.

The 1886 revelation mentions "conditions" of the law that "must be obeyed." Verse seven of section 132 discusses the *con-*

---

145. John Taylor, in *Journal of Discourses*, 26 vols. (Liverpool: F. D. Richards 1855–86), 24:229; italics added.

ditions of the *law* and plurality of wives is not mentioned, but the need for proper authority through the "one" man is emphasized. The revelation refers to the new and everlasting covenant, which "cannot be abrogated." Brigham Young taught that people enter the new and everlasting covenant as they are baptized into the Church: "All Latter-day Saints enter *the New and Everlasting Covenant* when they enter this Church."[146]

The 1886 revelation discusses commandments that "must be obeyed" unless "revoked." The Book of Mormon teaches that God will "command His people" regarding their marriage arrangements (Jacob 2:27, 30). Accordingly, Church members believe that monogamy could be commanded at times, revoking the practice of polygamy, just as polygamy could be commanded at other times, revoking monogamy as the divinely expected marital standard. Latter-day Saints embrace *continuous revelation* as the key in revealing these commandments: "We believe all that God has revealed, all that He does now reveal, and we believe that He will yet reveal many great and important things pertaining to the Kingdom of God" (Articles of Faith 1:9). Church members trust that through the process of *continuous revelation*, God commanded the practice of plural marriage in 1852, though no written revelation to that effect was ever circulated.

The divine process that produced the 1886 revelation to John Taylor was *continuous revelation*. Church members might argue that that revelation did not, and could not, signal an end to additional *continuous revelation* being received by the "one" man regarding plural marriage. Nor should it be considered to be the "final word" regarding the topics it discusses. The process of *continuous revelation* would always be active allowing additional divine communication to be received by prophets after John Taylor, like Wilford Woodruff, who would serve as the "one" man in 1889, 1890, and beyond.

146. Brigham Young, in *Journal of Discourses*, 12:230, May 17, 1868.

THE 1886 REVELATION TO JOHN TAYLOR		
	Fundamentalist Interpretation	Church Interpretation
The *Law*	"Law" of plural marriage	Law of celestial marriage
***Conditions* of the Law**	Always requires plural marriage	Always requires proper authority
New and Everlasting *Covenant*	Always requires plural marriage	Includes all covenants entered into through baptism and other ordinances
Doing the *Works* of Abraham	Must include plural marriage	Some of Abraham's works are not authorized or commanded today including sacrificing burnt offerings and plural marriage
Commandments	Plural marriage is a commandment that *cannot* be suspended or revoked	Plural marriage is a commandment that may be suspended or revoked

Latter-day Saints also reason that the fundamentalist interpretation of John Taylor's 1886 revelation would still require proper priesthood authority to implement. No one has suggested that the revelation alone could authorize any priesthood holder to seal marriages (either monogamist or polygamist) without the authority of the "one" man.

Possibly the greatest significance of the 1886 revelation stems not from what it says, but from the reaction of some Church leaders to its existence. In the 1920s and 1930s, it would be referred to as a "scrap of paper" and "a pretended revelation," with suggestions that it didn't even exist. In response, Mormon fundamentalists would rally in opposition to the perceived cover-up.

3. *Mormon fundamentalists believe that The Church of Jesus Christ of Latter-day Saints is the "house of God" that the "one mighty and strong" (mentioned in D&C 85:7) will "set in order."*

Of all scripture, no single verse is referred to more often by Mormon fundamentalists than Doctrine & Covenants 85:7:

> And it shall come to pass that I, the Lord God, will send *one mighty and strong*, holding the scepter of power in his hand, clothed with light for a covering, whose mouth shall utter words, eternal words; while his bowels shall be a fountain of truth, *to set in order the house of God,* and *to arrange by lot the inheritances* of the saints whose names are found, and the names of their fathers, and of their children, enrolled in the book of the law of God (italics added).

Joseph Smith wrote this verse on November 27, 1832, as part of a letter to W. W. Phelps, in response to disobedience among Church members in Jackson County, Missouri. In it he warned that if the problems were not resolved, the Lord would send "one mighty and strong" with two duties to perform in Zion (Independence, Missouri):

(1) to set in order the house of God, and
(2) to arrange by lot the inheritances of the saints

Mormon fundamentalists usually ignore the second duty all together, but it is a key to understanding the first.

Looking at the city plat of Zion sent to W. W. Phelps in 1833 shows that before the second responsibility of arranging "inheritance lots" for the Saints could be accomplished, the temple lot would need to be surveyed. This is because all of the boundaries of the "inheritance lots" parallel the central lots where the temple complex (of twelve buildings) will be constructed.

Reviewing the references to "house of God" in the Doctrine and Covenants shows them all to be referring to a physical building, usually a temple.[147] Accordingly, to *set in order* the *house of God* is simply referring to surveying the temple, which obviously must occur before the "one mighty and strong" can carry out his second important duty of arranging the lots.

Mormon fundamentalists strongly reject this obvious interpretation. Lifting this prophecy from its context, they assert the "house of God" mentioned was referring to The Church of Jesus Christ of Latter-day Saints headquartered in Salt Lake City, Utah, at least 150 years later. They also claim that through the efforts of the "one mighty and strong" mentioned, Mormon fundamentalists will be vindicated and the practice of plural marriage restored. A sweeping transformation of the mother church is also anticipated. Fundamentalist writer Ogden Kraut

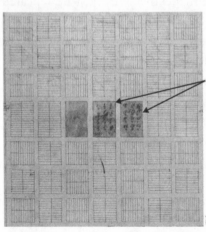

The temple complex (the "house of God") must be surveyed ("set in order") before any inheritance lots could be "arranged"

Joseph Smith sent this plat of Zion to Church leaders in Jackson County, Missouri on June 25, 1833

---

147. References to the "house of God" found in the Doctrine and Covenants are 45:18, 88:119, 88:129, 88:130, 88:136, 109:8, and 138:58.

summarized this hope and perspective: "The setting in order of the House of God will be a greater event than the Restoration... The miracles will be greater, the number of converts will be more numerous; the power and wealth of the Saints will be richer; and Zion—the New Jerusalem—will finally be built."[148]

A review of the beliefs of nineteenth-century Church leaders demonstrates that no early priesthood authorities embraced any notions similar to current fundamentalist traditions regarding the "one mighty and strong." Neither does the scripture, when kept within its context, seem to justify such expansive expectations.

4. Mormon fundamentalists believe that only certain words can be used to confer priesthood authority during ordinations and that any variation results in a defection ordination.

Many Mormon fundamentalists believe that only one method of priesthood conferral is acceptable and that any variation from that single process results in a defective ordination. Subsequently, ordinances performed by that man with the defective ordination are ineffective and must be repeated by someone who was himself ordained according to the pattern accepted by the fundamentalists.

It is true that over the decades since Joseph Smith's death, different opinions have existed concerning the wording used to confer priesthood authority, as well as the strictness that must also be followed. During the administration of Joseph F. Smith (1901–1918), the general policy was to first *confer* the priesthood and then *ordain* to the individual offices or callings within that priesthood.

However, the next President of the Church, Heber J. Grant (serving from 1918–1945), altered the official policy, specifying that a direct ordination to an office in the Aaronic or

148. Ogden Kraut, *The One Mighty and Strong* (Salt Lake City: Pioneer Press, 1991), 136–37.

Melchizedek Priesthood was all that was required and that conferring of the priesthood was redundant, and perhaps a presumptuous part of the ordinance. During President George Albert Smith's administration (1945–1951), he cautiously removed specificity in the ordinances as a general policy, thereby permitting either form to be used. When David 0. McKay assumed the presidency in 1951, he reverted to the form followed during Joseph F. Smith's administration, which method is still being followed as the official Church policy.

Mormon fundamentalists generally assume that Joseph F. Smith's approach is the only acceptable method and that all direct ordinations to a priesthood office (Heber J. Grant's approach) were ineffective.

Nevertheless, a review of the terminology used to confer priesthood authority during the nineteenth century shows a variety of words and methods were used. No one approach was universally applied and Church leaders were not adamant about one specific method. It appears that direct ordinations to a priesthood office (as Heber J. Grant knew) were the most common as proxy priesthood ordinations in LDS temples utilized this method.

A concern for proper verbiage predated both Presidents Joseph F. Smith and Heber J. Grant. George Q. Cannon, a member of the First Presidency in 1894, wrote:

> Ordaining to the Priesthood. We have been asked by several persons whether in ordaining a brother, it is right to confer the Priesthood first and then ordain him to the particular office to which he is called, or to directly ordain him to that office in the Priesthood. That is in ordaining a man an Elder, should the one officiating say: "I confer upon you the Melchizedek Priesthood and ordain you an Elder," or "I ordain you an Elder in the Melchizedek [Priesthood]" or whatever the office conferred may be?

> So far as we know, the Lord has revealed no par-
> ticular form or words to be used in the ceremony of
> ordination to the Priesthood as he has done in the rite of
> baptism, neither has he given any direct instructions on
> the point presented by the inquirers. Certain it is that
> both forms have been and are being used by those of-
> ficiated, ordained in either way. Consequently, we are of
> the opinion that both are acceptable to him, and will be
> until it pleases him to give the Church further light on
> the subject, either by direct revelation or by inspiring his
> servants of the First Presidency of the Church to direct
> exactly what shall be said.[149]

Heber J. Grant recognized that President Joseph F. Smith's biases were in favor of the newer confer/ordain approach. However, when he became President of the Church, President Grant felt to return to the older, more established terminology taught in the earlier days of the Church of ordaining directly to office in the Priesthood. To avoid confusion, the terminology was standardized by President McKay returning to Joseph's F. Smith's method, but that process did not nullify previous ordinations that utilized a different approach.

A review of priesthood ordinations during Church history fails to support the extreme interpretation held by many Mormon fundamentalists today.

5. Mormon fundamentalists seem to be guided by a different spirit than that followed by LDS Church members.

In looking at the types of individuals that might be attracted to Mormon fundamentalism, several situations seem common. First, there are women who might otherwise struggle to find a husband. They may be divorced or beyond common marriageable ages and deeply desiring some level of companionship. Janet Bennion assessed: "Women, particularly, search-

---

149. George Q. Cannon, *Juvenile Instructor*, 29 (1894)114.

ing for a way to remove the stigmata of divorce, abandonment, spinsterhood, single parenthood, or widowhood, are seeking polygynous and fundamentalist networks to solve these socio-economic crises.... Many more women may be willing to share a good man rather than gain full use of a loser or have no man at all."[150] Issues of authority and faith may become less important to a woman starved for attention, facing an uncertain future alone.

Second are "intellectuals" who are genuinely convinced that plural marriage is still commanded and that authority is still available to seal polygamous unions. Such individuals are usually familiar with the teachings given by Church leaders between 1852 and 1890 regarding plural marriage and other topics and keep their gospel focus firmly there.

A third group is comprised of people who might be gently characterized as "religious tumbleweeds." Many of them come from other religions, sometimes having actively participated in several before being baptized into The Church of Jesus Christ of Latter-day Saints. After a few years as Church members, they become dissatisfied and search fundamentalist theology, partaking of plural marriage. Not uncommonly, after a few more years as a Mormon fundamentalist, they become disaffected again, joining some other religious movement or becoming an "independent."

The fourth type involves fanatics and extremists who adopt the Mormon fundamentalist agenda. In 1952, Samuel W. Taylor, well-known author and sometimes LDS curmudgeon, wrote: "[The] basic trouble of Fundamentalists is that they attract the screwball fringe."[151] Militant and often destructive, this type of fundamentalist, whether called Bin Laden, Laf-

---

150. Janet Bennion, *Desert Patriarchy: Mormon and Mennonite Communities in the Chihuahua Valley* (Tucson: University of Arizona Press, 2004), 15, 185.

151. Samuel W. Taylor, "Trip to Short Creek August 1952." Mimeographed copy in author's possession.

ferty, or LeBaron, is sometimes willing to kill and maim in the name of their god.

In my experience studying Mormon fundamentalism, I have come to believe that three factors often combine to comfort adherents in their current beliefs as they find themselves outside The Church of Jesus Christ of Latter-day Saints. First among these is *sincerity*. Fundamentalists sometimes assume that in light of their sincere and intense desires to serve God, He would not allow them to go astray. Joseph Musser displayed this feeling in a journal entry dated March 11, 1935: "Those of us who feel the need of more definite direction from the Lord should take courage in the feeling that since we have dedicated all unto God, and are executing all our energies to keep his commandments, the Lord must be pleased with our course, else he would set us right; no good father will permit his children who want to do right to go far astray."[152]

Musser's opinion seems to reflect a bit of naiveté, believing that sincere desires and dedication would automatically shield him and his fellow polygamists from deception. Throughout the world today we find seemingly sincere individuals following diverse gods and theologies.

The scriptures inform us that there are unseen forces dedicated to deceiving sincere people. They tell us that Satan "maketh war with the saints of God, and encompasseth them round about" (D&C 76:29); "Behold, verily I say unto you, that there are many spirits which are false spirits, which have gone forth in the earth, deceiving the world. And also Satan hath sought to deceive you, that he might overthrow you" (D&C 50:2–3; see also 46:7, 52:14). Falsehoods can be espoused with the same level of sincerity as truth can be embraced.

A second prominent element is *tradition*. Each of the fundamentalist factions possesses a powerful tradition regarding

152. Joseph Musser Journals, for date, originals in Church Archives; copy of holograph in possession of the author.

the past and present identity of who holds the proper authority to seal eternal marriages. Of course, these traditions, though embraced by hundreds or thousands of individuals, lead their followers to several different men, each esteemed as the "one" holding the keys. The problem is that acclamation or the formation of a well-accepted tradition does not guarantee that truth is part of the process. The scriptures warn: "That wicked one cometh and taketh away light and truth, through disobedience, from the children of men, and because of the tradition of their fathers" (D&C 93:39).

A third component empowering the choices of modern polygamists is *personal revelation*. It appears that most Mormon fundamentalists, no matter what their background, have one thing in common. They have a "burning in their bosoms" or have received some kind of a witness in their "hearts" that what they are doing is right. Sometimes open visions of angelic visitations are shared.

These personal revelations are gifts from the spirit that Mormon fundamentalists follow and are different from the spiritual directives received by members of The Church of Jesus Christ of Latter-day Saints in many ways. Both spirits provide their followers with powerful emotions, sometimes moving them to tears. Both spirits prompt their adherents in other hidden but undeniable ways. Both spirits generate unique feelings that sustain their disciples through trials. Both spirits move their advocates to obey God's will, no matter the sacrifice.

However, significant differences exist. Most obvious is that the spirit of Mormon fundamentalism has not prompted fundamentalists to do missionary work (or temple work), which Church members are still guided to do. Fundamentalists are provoked to focus their energies inward, often producing an isolationist mentality and closed society. This self-focus is understandable. It produces an effective response in confronting persecution and helps fathers as they distribute their limited resources to expanding numbers of wives and children. How can patriarchs also juggle missionary work or proxy work for the dead with all their family responsibilities?

Perhaps this dissimilarity regarding missionary work is unimportant. Or possibly it is just the tip of the spiritual iceberg, an incongruity that symbolizes much more than a simple disparity in administrative policies.

The spirit followed by most fundamentalist polygamists teaches that polygamy is so important, that no additional sacrifices from the modern polygamist in the form of missionary work are required. *A review of the scriptures and prophetic pronouncements shows that this represents a new doctrine, unheard of in the times of Joseph Smith and Brigham Young.* The practice of plural marriage never exempted early Church members from preaching the gospel. How could it? In God's eternal plan, gathering the elect in the last days is infinitesimally more important than polygamy. Redeeming the dead is equally more imperative. And it seems that the Spirit burning in the hearts of monogamist Latter-day Saints understands the eternal importance of these priorities.

The Lord warned: "And again, I will give unto you a pattern in all things, that ye may not be deceived; for Satan is abroad in the land, and he goeth forth deceiving the nations" (D&C 52:14). God's pattern includes the need for missionary work (see Mark 16:15, D&C 18:28, 34:5, 68:8 etc.).

How do we discern the difference between personal revelation from God and that from a false spirit? The Lord instructed Joseph Smith saying He would answer our prayers in a specific way: "Yea, behold, I will tell you in your *mind* and in your *heart*, by the Holy Ghost, which shall come upon you and which shall dwell in your heart" (D&C 8:2; italics added). "Behold, I say unto you, that you must study it out in your mind;

then you must ask me if it be right, and if it is right I will cause that your bosom shall burn within you; therefore, you shall feel that it is right" (D&C 9:8).

Without proper study, our "minds" will not be positioned to hear God's voice and our hearts will be left exposed to false spirits. So many Mormon fundamentalists seem to have studied little regarding their own history, their leaders' claims to priesthood keys, and even Joseph Smith's teachings on priesthood authority. If they subsequently allow a heart-witness to override their unawareness or to nullify the doubts that exist in their minds, they can be deceived.

6. *Section 132 of the Doctrine and Covenants emphasizes the importance of proper priesthood authority in sealing eternal marriage (monogamous or polygamous), which is sometimes ignored by modern polygamists.*

In looking at eternal sealings and the plurality of wives, it appears that Heavenly Father anticipated this day. He provided His followers with section 132, which contains specific instructions regarding eternal sealings, instructions that are in some ways unique among all scripture. This is because after God introduces the concept that "one" man holds the keys, He discusses four different situations and how they would be affected by the sealing authority that has just been restored to the earth. The Lord provides us with specific examples so that we will not be confused or mislead. Section 132 may be the only place in scripture where Heavenly Father goes to such lengths to explain a new idea.

The first set of circumstances described is found in verse thirteen. God observes that "*everything* that is in the world, whether it be ordained of men, by thrones, or principalities, or powers, or things of name, whatsoever they may be, that are not by me or by my word, saith the Lord, shall be thrown down, and shall not remain after men are dead" (italics added). Starting with the basics, the Lord explains that worldly "things," even if highly revered by men and women and endorsed by kings and presidents on earth, will not persist after death. The message is clear that mortal men and women have no power in and of themselves to create enduring objects or affairs.

Next in verses fifteen to seventeen, the Lord picks out one situation that is very important to Him and His children and addresses *marriage* specifically: "If a man marry him a wife in the world, and he marry her not by me nor by my word, and he covenant with her so long as he is in the world and she with him, their covenant and marriage are not of force when they are dead." He also specifies the eternal destination of those individuals: "[They] neither marry nor are given in marriage; but are appointed angels in heaven... [and] remain separately and singly, without exaltation, in their saved condition, to all eternity."

The third scenario described seems to have been included particularly for our day and perhaps even as an explicit message to modern polygamists. It declares that even marrying with sincerity, utilizing the right wordage, and exercising a full hope of eternal union, are not enough. The authorization of the "one" man, the key holder, is still absolutely required:

> And again, verily I say unto you, if a man marry a wife, and make a covenant with her for time and for all eternity, if that covenant is not by me or by my word, which is my law, and is not sealed by the Holy Spirit of promise, through him whom I have anointed and appointed unto this power, then it is not valid neither of force when they are out of the world, because they are not joined by me, saith the Lord, neither by my word; when they are out of the world it cannot be received there, because the angels and the gods are appointed there, by whom they cannot pass; they cannot, therefore, inherit my glory; for my house is a house of order, saith the Lord God. (D&C 132:18.)

These first three illustrations go from general to specific in relating the importance of the sealing authority and the "one" man who controls it on earth. In the first example, the Lord tells us generally that without sealing authority, things will not persist beyond death. The second addresses marriage only. The third focuses on marriage again, but this time even more precisely. (It appears that Heavenly Father is trying to help us understand a very important principle.) In the third situation, the Lord further explains that even marriage ceremonies that are contracted by earnest individuals who possess a hope of eternal union and even implement the words of the temple sealing ordinance, will end at death.

The fourth example is different from the other three. It discusses the blessings that are available if the sealing authority is implemented according to God's word as marriage covenants are made. Thereafter, the Lord extends promises that the union can be eternal, and offers additional blessings that transcend our comprehension, if the husband and wife are obedient. In short, verses nineteen and twenty explain Heavenly Father's promise of exaltation to a monogamist couple who are sealed by proper authority and live worthily:

> And again, verily I say unto you, if a man marry a wife by my word, which is my law, and by the new and everlasting covenant, and it is sealed unto them by the Holy Spirit of promise, by him who is anointed, unto whom I have appointed this power and the keys of this priesthood... shall inherit thrones, kingdoms, principalities, and powers, dominions, all heights and depths... and they shall pass by the angels, and the gods, which are set there, to their exaltation and glory in all things, as hath been sealed upon their heads, which glory shall be a fulness and a continuation of the seeds forever and ever.
>
> Then shall they be gods, because they have no end; therefore shall they be from everlasting to everlasting,

> because they continue; then shall they be above all, be-
> cause all things are subject unto them. Then shall they
> be gods, because they have all power, and the angels are
> subject unto them.

There is no greater promise in all scripture. Indeed, no greater promise could be made by anyone, even God himself. Mormon fundamentalists and LDS Church members seek these blessings, but their chosen paths course through very different terrain. Are modern polygamists keepers of the true way? Or are they unauthorized practitioners of principles previously suspended by God through continuous revelation to His prophets on earth? Time and eternity will tell.

About the Author

This is Brian C. Hales' third book dealing with Mormon fundamentalist polygamy. In 1992 he co-authored *The Priesthood of Modern Polygamy, an LDS Perspective.* Fourteen years later he wrote *Modern Polygamy and Mormon Fundamentalism: The Generations After the Manifesto,* which received the Best Book of 2007 award from the John Whitmer Historical Association Award. Brian works as an anesthesiologist at the Davis Hospital and Medical Center in Layton, Utah, where he has served as the Director of the Anesthesia Department and Chairman of Surgical Services. He has also served as the Medical Director of the Davis Surgical Center and President of the Davis County Medical Society in 2009. An active member of the Church of Jesus Christ of Latter-day Saints and a former full-time missionary, he is the webmaster of mormonfundamentalism.com, a website dedicated to providing viewers with a historical and doctrinal examination of Mormon fundamentalist beliefs. Brian has presented at the Mormon History Association meetings, Sunstone Symposiums, and John Whitmer Historical Association meetings on polygamy-related topics. His articles have also been published in *Dialogue, A Journal of Mormon Thought* and the *Journal of Mormon History.* In addition to his historical works, Brian has authored three books on doctrinal themes entitled *The Veil* (Cedar Fort, 2000), *Trials* (Cedar Fort, 2002), and *Light* (Cedar Fort, 2004). He is the father of four children.

SETTING THE RECORD STRAIGHT SERIES

MORMONS & MASONS

GILBERT W. SCHARFFS, Ph.D

MORMONS POLYGAMY

JESSIE L. EMBRY

BLACKS THE MORMON PRIESTHOOD

MARCUS H. MARTINS, Ph.D.

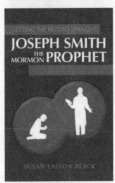

JOSEPH SMITH THE MORMON PROPHET

SUSAN EASTON BLACK

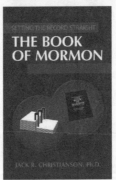

THE BOOK OF MORMON

JACK R. CHRISTIANSON, Ph.D.

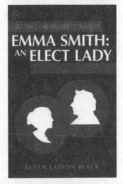

EMMA SMITH: AN ELECT LADY

SUSAN EASTON BLACK

MORMON TEMPLES

DEAN L. LARSEN

THE WORD OF WISDOM

STEVEN C. HARPER, Ph.D.

JOSEPH SMITH: PRESIDENTIAL CANDIDATE

ARNOLD K. GARR, Ph.D.

To learn more about these and other Millennial Press titles,
visit www.millennialpress.com. Available wherever books are sold.